Horizons

A Legacy

By

Amelia Morse

To my Family

Paperback ISBN: 978-1-910088-26-5
Ebook ISBN: 978-1-910088-27-2

Published by SifiPublishing 2015

SIFIPUBLISHING
WWW.SIFIPUBLISHING.CO.UK

PV24

Contents

"We will show them Our Signs on the horizon and within themselves until it is clear for them that it is the truth."

Qur'an (41:53) Translation by Abdalhaqq and Aisha Bewley

Preface

"The world is divided into people who see a horizon and want to look over it and those who see a horizon and feel it will keep them safe. I am one of those who want to look over the next horizon. Life is a journey and there is another horizon you go over at the end of it."
Freya Stark

1970

I could see nothing but flat desert and sky in every direction. There were two camel trains in the distance and little tornados of dust making elegant spirals into the sky. I had woken from a nap in the back of the landrover, while the two men were lying in the sand underneath the car investigating the damage. It seemed the 'big end' had gone and we were stuck in the middle of the great Dasht-a-Kevir, the salt desert between Tehran and Herat.

It was my first journey east. We were on our way to Afghanistan, which was still ruled by King Zahir Shah and was relatively peaceful and progressive. Jake and I had a shop in World's End in Chelsea and were going to buy carpets, jewellery and 'other things' that were fashionable in swinging London in the early 1970's. I was 24 and had already travelled to Morocco, but after the initial culture shock, although exotic, it eventually felt tame. Now we had driven through Yugoslavia, dined in Bulgaria, already Slavic and boisterous but still with a European familiarity, to Istanbul where we visited the Topkapi Museum. There the beautifully painted miniatures promised a wild strangeness – places built by Ottomans and Moghuls with names like Orhan, Babur and Timur. Once we had crossed the Bosphorus, we were in Asia and the adventure really began. We dipped down into the south of Turkey and sat with fishermen above a beach in Side, smoking hashish amongst Roman ruins, gazing at the millions of stars, and contemplating the immensity of the universe. As soon as we had drawn breath, we drove on through to Lake Van where the church made a strong impression on me. The Muslims had defaced the hand-painted saints. The guide explained that to the Christians it was desecration, but to the Muslims it was putting things right. I had no ideas about Islam at that time but it struck me that here were people who cared about the details of their beliefs. They had taken the trouble to remove what was to them a profanity but carefully left the rest of the artist's work in its entirety. It made sense. I had always disliked the faces painted in Christian churches, with their either pained or goody-goody expressions. How did they know what the prophets and saints looked like anyway? It seemed sensible to leave it to the imagination. After those thoughts, we drove on and tried to cross into Syria to see Aleppo, but the border guards would only allow us to pass for a day, and so we just saw the great red walls. On through to Iran via Tabriz and we whirled around Tehran in the crazy honking traffic and spent a very uncomfortable night sleeping on top of the landrover near the Caspian Sea, where the insects were three times the size of any I have ever seen before or since.

We stopped in Mashhad where I bought some turquoise stones which I thought would be an good investment, and we were caught in a sandstorm and hid in a dusty building until it passed. In a few minutes everything was covered in sand. It made me experientially aware that deserts hold few memories, because between the sun, sand and wind, all previous landmarks are quickly wiped away. They cease to exist. Mud houses crumble and disappear into the sand. Life seemed no longer solid or durable, as I had felt it in the safety of England. At the same time, I knew from my education that the desert is a clean clear place where men have gone for inspiration and clarity. As a schoolgirl, the film "Lawrence of Arabia" with Peter O'Toole crossing the desert with the Bedouin particularly enraptured me; I found the Bedouin more alluring than him, but I had ploughed my way through "The Seven Pillars of Wisdom" trying to extract some knowledge. When we said evening prayers in my house at school, my point of contemplation had been a picture on the wall, of an Arab lying in his tent in the sand dunes, with his horse at the entrance

Jake and Paul managed to get the car going and although it was ailing we struggled on to Herat. It was a tense drive because we were in danger of being stranded in that wilderness I had found so terribly romantic. I imagined us disappearing without any trace in the empty, unforgiving desert. I made a prayer and promised to do something for God if He got me out of this. Not that I did not admire and love the stark beauty of the desert, I just did not want to end my days there, yet.

My prayer was answered very quickly. We reached Kabul, by some miracle, and we started to bargain for carpets with a delightful shopkeeper, whom we named 'friend and brother' because he always prefixed the bargains he gave us with – 'I am your friend and brother, I will give you a good price'. He tempted me with a small silver ring set with a beautiful blue lapis lazuli stone. The shank of the ring had a small hole through which he said you could see the Ka'aba in Mecca, but 'only if you are a Muslim'. I do not think I had much idea what the Ka'aba was, but intrigued by his reverence for it, I wanted the ring. 'Friend and brother' would not sell it to me for any price. Equally impressive was the way that, in the middle of the sale about which he obviously cared, he would leap up, cross the shop, put down a mat and pray. Then he would come back with renewed energy and bargain even harder. We spent many hours in the shop buying carpets and everyday they would provide us with lunch spread out on the floor. Afterwards any food left was given to the local policeman on the street outside; they explained that he was paid next to nothing by the government and this kept him well-fed and vigilant, over their shop at least. The poverty that these people cheerfully put up with made a great impression upon me; I was not used to it, and it seemed not to degrade them as it did the few beggars I had come across in England, who were often drunk.

We spent some time in Kabul buying the wares we wanted to take back to London, and then decided to go up to Mazar-Sharif and on to Balkh. By now we were aware of the competition between the Russians and Americans; firstly, to woo the country with aid such as building good roads – one of which we took advantage of on this trip north; and secondly, to occupy it by force. This, even as I write in 2014, has proven over the years, futile. It seems historically impossible to conquer, both by western and eastern invaders.

Balkh was the scene of a more remarkable meeting that I must relate. The journey itself was magical, partly enhanced by the fact that we took some mescalin in the Salang Pass, a beautiful place with a rushing river full of trout. Some young Afghani boys appeared out of nowhere, and 'tickled' the trout for us and we built a campfire and barbequed them. There was not a soul in sight but we could see the traces of the carefully extinguished ashes of the nomad's cooking fires. As we were wondering what we would have for pudding, some more boys appeared with a bucket of delicious fresh yoghurt that we mixed with some peaches, honey and almonds we had in the car. I have never forgotten that pudding; it is still a favourite and brings back memories of the Salang Pass.

Later, on the high wild mountain road, we saw extraordinary wandering *'malungs'*, the Afghani name for a '*majdoob*' or dervish. One, in particular, was striding along the empty mountain pass, in just a loincloth. We stopped and gave him some food, asking him if he needed anything. He shook his head and pointed to his chest that was pierced with scores of safety pins, indicating he would like some more. It seemed a strange desire for someone who apparently had absolutely nothing. We had none to give him. We passed Buddhist shrines with little homemade flags fluttering above them, and nomadic Kuchi tribe people with their big dogs and camels. I admired the Kuchi women who wore the stunning black embroidered dresses so fashionable in London at the time. They had a tremendous air of power and freedom, not present in the grey burka clad women of Kabul, whom I never met to speak to.

When we arrived in Mazar-Sharif, we took a painted lorry and stood in the back along with other Afghan travellers until we reached Balkh. The faces, even in that small space, were evidence that we were in the centre of Asia. There were flat slit-eyed round-faced Mongolians, long faced hawk-nosed Arabs with high cheekbones, darker more swarthy Persians. Balkh was a sandy, deserted place with the vestiges of a great city. A guide attached himself to us and took us to greet a man who was sitting at the foot of the ruins. The man seemed to be no more than middle-aged, although Afghanis are sturdy people who often do not show their years. Alone, I would probably have passed by arrogantly thinking he was a beggar or a threat, but we followed our guide's example greeting him with respect since he was obviously someone special. The man greeted us courteously and we sat around him. As with the wandering malung we asked him if there was anything he needed that we could give him, passing him some gifts of food we had with us. He thanked us and smiled replying that Allah provided his needs. He said the little stream he was sitting by gave him water, and the date palm above him shade and food; the rest, people like us brought him. Although he said he had never travelled, he knew everything that happened in the world – how a man had gone to the moon and about President Kennedy. He wore a scruffy suit jacket over his Afghani *shawwal khemis,* and out of his pocket he drew some scraps of paper, saying that these were his only and most precious possessions. I was somehow able to understand every word he said, although I had only picked up a few words of Farsi during our stay in Kabul.

After a while I decided to leave the men and wander up onto the ruins. Very soon I heard angry shouts, and the wild gesticulations told me I should not be where I was. I returned rather ashamed and embarrassed and was told that the place where I had chosen to wander was an ancient graveyard, and I must not step on the graves. Sand, wind and the passage of time had wiped out, what I later learnt was the ancient city Marco Polo described as 'a noble and great seat of learning'; and the birthplace of Jalaluddin Rumi, the great sufi shaykh, whose 'Mathnawi' I was to discover later.

I forgot all these experiences quickly when I tried to pick up my old life in England, and decide what was my next goal. But then, one day not so long after my return, sitting on the floor of my shop in Chelsea over a cup of coffee, I found myself relating the story of the encounter to the man we had left in charge while we were travelling. Although he was one of our Chelsea friends, I recognized a similar quality in him to the man in Balkh. There was something beyond the outward form that they had in common; he knew something in the same way as the man far away in Afghanistan. I started to tell my story, and in the telling of it, I became aware that the meeting had been very important to me. My friend was immediately very interested and his companion, who was in the shop at the time, said to me as I was leaving: "Perhaps you should consider that now is the time to stop travelling outwardly and travel inwardly." They had reopened a door to an unseen world that, after my childhood, I had thought could only be accessed through drugs or by travel to far-off places.

Horizons

A Legacy

Chapter I

Wiltshire 1998

"The unexamined life is no life for a man"
Socrates

The Shepherds Cottage is a small thatched cottage perched high up on the chalky Wiltshire Downs. It had been the final home of my grandmother, Marly Morse. The cottage was always a point of surety in a somewhat insecure childhood; one of those ideal places - with its lovely garden and small white wicket gate. My grandmother and her companion, Mary, converted the cottage that had previously belonged to a hill shepherd, into a comfortable home after the end of the Second World War. One entered the house through a white stable door, straight into a small but adequate kitchen where there was a little table on which they ate most of their meals. Passing through the kitchen on the right was my grandmother's bedroom, which was at the head of the long narrow passage that made the house resemble a ship. Its narrowness made it hard not to brush against old warm coats that hung on the coat rack on the left. The next room on the right was the tiny bedroom that had been mine and seemed unchanged apart from piles of boxes. The bookshelf was still lined with a miniature Beatrix Potter collection I had subsequently rejected for pony books like "Black Beauty" and "Rosina Copper", which took up their place alongside them. An ancient black upright typewriter Mary had given me when I was about ten for my 'office', held its peace, replaced many years ago by computers. Touching and smelling those old things brought my early years flooding back. I remembered my grandmother reading bedtime stories, while I lay in the narrow Heal's bed, its eiderdown secured with a soft blanket to prevent it slipping off. She taught me the Lord's prayer and to believe in God, and I would drift off to sleep to the sound of the sheep bleating on the Downs. It was a secure well-ordered world that I had loved as a child, very different from home in London with my mother which was much more chaotic and bohemian, and often in conflict with theirs. I never really understood the conflict, but it worried me and when I grew up I decided to reject them all and find my own way.

The next stop on the right was a tiny lavatory with magazines like 'The Lady' and old gardening and seed catalogues, and adjacent, a small bathroom where my grandmother would have her morning bath in rainwater, collected from the roof. In the fifties, the bathroom with its beige tiles and stainless steel mixer taps had seemed to me terribly luxurious and modern, even though it was small. I could still picture my grandmother, sitting afterwards, like a duchess in front of her dressing table with a plastic shoulder guard protecting her clothes from the loose powder she dabbed on her nose with a swan's down powder puff. The incongruity was somehow very dear, odd and very English!

At the other end of the passage was Mary's bedroom – full of tools and even a workbench, where she did her carpentry work. On the left hand side of the passage, the large spacious sitting room ran almost the full length of the cottage and had a door that opened on to the garden. Here box hedges surrounded the small lawn and there was birdbath, which my brother and I used as a paddling pool, when we were very small. A fig tree, in the summer laden with purple figs, was their pride and joy. In the autumn in London we would receive parcels of carefully packed figs wrapped in tissue paper. The wicket gate led out on to the village green and was fiercely guarded by some rather threatening geese, which would run after us as we crossed the path. They no longer seemed to be in evidence. On the other side of the green was the vegetable garden where Mary's school friend, Rosellen, lived in a small wooden cabin and came over to cook for them.

Almost 30 years later, in 1998, Mary died at the ripe old age of 98, leaving the cottage and its contents to my brother and I. We dutifully arranged and attended the funeral and then had the task of clearing out the house for sale. My grandmother died in 1967, since when I had not seen much of Mary nor visited the cottage. Our relationship with her had been for the sake of my grandmother. These days the past had less and less bearing on my life; I no longer thought much about my childhood as I was busy bringing up my own children in a very different world. Mary's increasing frailty but fierce independence and dislike of interference from well-meaning neighbours, had meant that over the years the place had become covered in dust and piled up debris. I imagined she had led a rather Miss Havisham existence caught in the time warp mourning my grandmother's demise, but perhaps that was unfair, and just a way of assuaging my guilt for not visiting her more frequently. The advantage was that during that time very little had changed. There it all was – exactly the same as I remembered it.

Once I had cleared some of the rooms, I climbed the sturdy steps someone had made, probably Mary, up to the attic in my grandmother's room. Amongst old suitcases and boxes I came upon a brown envelope neatly labelled *"For my grandchildren"*. What a strange thing! It was as if it had been waiting for me all those years until I was ready to be interested. I was not sure I was, even now, but I packed it amongst the other things I had chosen to keep – photograph albums and other memories of childhood; the soft merino wool blanket from Harrods that had stopped the eiderdown slipping off my bed; a china penguin; a small upright 'vanity' chest with bone labels on the drawers, saying 'jewellery, veils, ribbons, lace, gloves'. I would have a look when I had more time.

It was not for another ten years that I finally looked again at the manuscript. I was busy with my own life and, I suppose, still a little reluctant to delve into a past that I thought I had left behind. Finally, when moving house again and sorting through my papers, I came upon the yellowing typed pages. I decided I was curious to see if they would shed any light on who these people were that formed part of my matrix. Left to me from beyond the grave, the memoirs started a new phase of discovery.

My grandmother began:

*'When the first war came in **1914** we were very young and ready to change the way we lived, the way we loved and the way we hoped to be and do. By **1939** we were not so young, nor so ready to face changes and*

events that were even more dynamic. Like other women whose husbands and sons must go – mine both serving in the Navy – I had to make up my mind what part I must play in this great and terrible upheaval.'

My interest was caught. I was about to enter another world. My grandparents grew up in the late Victorian and Edwardian era; they lived through two terrible world wars that shattered life-as-they-had-known-it on a personal and a global level. My grandmother must have wanted to explain something and I felt to read her words was the least I could do to honour her memory. Now I was nearing my old age, I was rather fascinated to know the people who I had loved as a child, but then rejected in an effort to find my own way in life. This would be like forensic detective work into, not only what made me who I was, but into the events that made up the world in which we all live today.

My grandmother rather summed up anyone's life. At some point one had to make one's mind up what part one would play in the great upheaval of life. I had loved my grandmother with a child's uncritical eyes but knew how she had irritated my much more adventurous mother. I could recognise now, that with age, one is less likely to change, and wondered, perhaps, if she had become trapped in a role that even she, in spite of the appearance of security and comfort, found cramping. I hoped to discover a human being whom I had loved in my early years within these pages.

Chapter 2

The Leeds Family

Sir George William Leeds m 1797 Maria Sanderson
born 11th Nov 1773 Croxton Park
(created **1st Bart** Dec 1812)
died 1817
dau Rev William, of Morpeth

- .Elizabeth
- Anne
- Sir Joseph Edward (2nd Bart)
- **George**
  m 1850 Anne Place,
  dau Thomas Dumayne
  - Emily
  - Florence Mary
  - **Rev William Howard**
    m 1886 Ethel Beatrice
    dau of Charles Henry Perkins
    - **Mary Faith Leeds (Marly)**
    - Gabriel Francis Leeds (Din)

'I, Mary Faith Leeds or Marly as everyone called me, was born in ***1889****. My father, the Reverend William Howard Leeds died in* ***1893*** *when he was thrown from a horse in a hunting accident. I was four years old. His grandfather, Sir George William Leeds, owned* ***10,000*** *acres and two packs of hounds and had equipped a regiment to send to the Peninsular War in* ***1812*** *against Napoleon, for which he was made 1st Baronet of Croxton Park Cambridgeshire by King George III.'*

I remembered how my grandmother loved a title or, as she called it, someone with a 'handle to his name', which she indeed had by the end of her life by virtue of my grandfather's bravery and service. We, especially my mother, always thought it rather tiresome of her to be so snobbish and insist that she was addressed as Lady Morse in restaurants and hotels.

Ethel Perkins, with Marly as a baby

Ethel's sister, San

'By the time my young attractive mother Ethel Beatrice (Perkins) was widowed after only seven years of marriage, all this wealth and property was long gone

and she was left at the age of twenty-seven, with two daughters to bring up on a vicar's pension. She rose to the challenge and moved to a tiny but charming house in Broadstairs, Kent. I spent a happy childhood there with my younger sister Gabriel, or Din as we all called her. We had the freedom to roam the fisherman's huts and sands searching in rock pools for shells and shrimps. My resourceful mother, in spite of having small means, managed to have some social life. Although it was practically unthought-of, in those Victorian days for a woman to go out at night alone, she came up with the novel idea of hiring a Bath chair, so she could visit her friends without seeming too scandalous.'

'Gags' and motor with author's mother Jane, as a girl

My mother adored her grandmother, 'Gags', saying she was full of fun and adventure, unlike the way she saw her own mother – my grandmother

'When I was eleven, my mother rather reluctantly had to give up her independent life and go and look after her own mother, in Addison Gardens in London. Grandma Leeds lived with her other daughter San, a professional violinist, who worked and so was unable to take sufficient care of her mother.

Grandma Leeds was a kind but very old-fashioned lady, who wore a little cap of Honiton lace, perched on the top of her head. She never seemed to take it off and was continuously making a new one. She ran her Victorian household with a rod of iron, and Din and I spent a lot of time in the kitchens listening to, and sympathising with, the servants' complaints about their lot in life. My mother had the privacy of her own sitting room but in comparison to the freedom of our lives at Broadstairs, this exclusively female household, with an aging and very strait-laced grandmother, was a somewhat stifling existence for us all. Holidays at Steyne in Bembridge in the Isle of Wight, with our cousins the Thornycroft family, were a welcome relief from all the restrictions.

Marly at Steyne

It was more than that – it was a blissful carefree existence to which we both kept returning for the rest of our lives. We could relax and indulge in sumptuous meals, run free along the beaches and lanes, splash barefoot on the beach and catch shrimps and prawns in the rock pools. And there were uncles and male cousins like the Sassoon's to play with and get to know. The Sassoon's were related through Theresa Sassoon, who was Hamo's sister. They were all sculptors and designers of boats and interesting and fun.'

As I read I recalled the 'bung' (bungalow) my grandmother later built in Bembridge, and how my brother and I had had equally pleasurable holidays in exactly the same way. It was a joy and freedom after life in Soho in London, where we lived with our mother, not uncomfortably, in a fourth floor flat. My grandmother must have relived her childhood through our eyes. I remembered the innocent pleasure of spending all summer on the Isle of Wight. The journey by steam-train to Portsmouth and short ferry crossing to Ryde were an adventure. Another little train took us on to Brading, St. Helens and then Bembridge, where we arrived slightly grimy and sooty, as one always did in the days of steam-trains, and the stationmaster greeted us like long lost friends. The air was fresh and clean and smelt of the sea. We would wander barefoot down Ducie Avenue to the beach hut where we kept all our swimming things and a small flat-bottomed boat. By the end of the summer our feet were so hardened to the pebbles we could run across them, much to the chagrin of our softer London friends who came to stay. We fished for mackerel with a line run from the back of a motor boat; shrimped in the rock pools with jam jars, holding our breath so that the transparent shrimps would not see us waiting for them to dart into the jar; learnt to ride on donkeys on the sand at low tide.

The author riding on beach at Bembridge

When we were older, we had sailing lessons at the Bembridge Sailing Club, after which with hearty appetites we filled our plates to overflowing from the buffet lunch they served. Then there were dances and first romances. Our childhood friends, a larger than life family of eight children, had a big, jolly house next door and came for the whole summer too; with them we acted Shakespeare plays and climbed trees, both of which they did extremely well and I found terrifying.

One of Marly's Minatures

'By 1914 when the war began I was quite an independent young woman. I had spent some time at art school and made a small income painting portraits and miniatures of acquaintances.

I even had a picture exhibited in The Royal

Academy. Sometimes my subjects invited me to stay with them while I worked on the portrait and we became friends. I went touring all over England and Scotland by motor-car; probably if I had had a father he would have frowned on this freedom, which was still considered quite daring. Influenced by my mother I took an interest in the suffragettes, going along to some of the meetings, but although I liked the people and sympathized with their ideas, I never took up the cause seriously myself. I went to a lecture by the great George Bernard Shaw, although that had been rather irritatingly and intolerantly interrupted by my friend's father, who stood up and declared: "Let's go – I can't stand any more of this damned chap's talk." In the house of a different friend, I once had the good fortune to have tea with Tolstoy. Unfortunately I remember that I said nothing of interest to him, other than to ask him which little iced cake to have. "The coffee one of course!" he replied. Life was interesting and fulfilling and although many of my friends were getting engaged, and we of course discussed marriage frequently, (I even had one or two proposals) I did not take it seriously. I was enjoying my independence too much and had not met anybody with whom I thought I could spend the rest of my days.'

I was impatient to get to the part about my grandfather. He interested me more because I remembered him much less well than my grandmother, and my mother adored him. He was a handsome man, familiar to me mostly from the photographs on the wall of my mother's room. He had Gregory Peck good looks and in his Admiral's uniform he had an air of perfect uprightness and manliness.

I do not think that men like my grandfather exist anymore. Their generation was dying out by the 1980's, and globalization and modern technology is gradually erasing the characteristics and individuality by which each nationality was once recognized.

My grandfather

One hears their clipped, well-pronounced English on the archive BBC newsreels; sees their wiry lean bodies in vintage films, fit with hard work, training and a war-rationed diet; they had the healthy morals of men who had suffered and served together, fighting a common enemy, and a deep love and respect for their fellows. They hardly ever expressed their feelings, I am sure they had them but their 'stiff upper lips' did not permit them to show any, and they grew up to learn to repress them. They were probably quite difficult to live with, since many of them after serving in the War were not accustomed to family life, and often they made their children's lives somewhat dismal, with little familiar affection. I do not say that was the case of my grandfather who, whenever we saw him, was warm and affectionate, but he had little opportunity to express it. When the Americans came over at the end of World War II to 'liberate' us, they brought a freedom and gaiety with them that the British lacked, but they also brought a flabbiness in character and physical build that is now universally predominant in life in 21st century Britain. By the time I was born, at the end of the Second World War, he and my grandmother were already leading separate lives. Seduced by fairy tales that always ended 'happily ever after', I was fascinated by what seemed to be elusive 'successful marriages', and often wondered what had gone wrong between them. Perhaps he had had a girl in every port, but somehow I doubted that, although an old friend of his from South Africa hinted that he had a girlfriend when he was living there. She said she always remembered him because he was extremely kind to her. She was very young and shy at the time, and he had noticed and helped her meet people at a function they had both attended. He was a beloved but distant figure in our childhood, and a great support to my single mother. When we were small children, Pom Pom, as we called him, visited the flat in Percy Street from time to time. I do not know where the name came from, but perhaps from the naval guns which were used in the First World War, or maybe he told us about them and my small brother repeated the sound. He read us Rudyard Kipling's stories, we both found the language a bit beyond our tender years, but appreciated the love he had for the stories and the time he spent with us.

Pom Pom with my brother Charlie

Juliet Morse, Anthony, Enid and Sydney Morse

Chapter 3

The Morse Family

'Anthony Morse, my future husband was born on 16th October 1892. I was three years older. His mother, Juliet Mary Tylor was a Quaker and a friend of Queen Victoria's fourth and most rebellious daughter, Princess Louise. Juliet's mother had been lady-in-waiting for a time in the Queen's household. The Princess was a clever and talented artist and she insisted on studying sculpture. Queen Victoria, who did not approve of such activities, eventually capitulated and engaged her first

tutor, Mary Thornycroft, a well-known sculptress who had done work for the Royal family. Mary, coincidentally, was the grandmother of my cousins the Thornycrofts and Sassoons. Princess Louise later married the Marquis of Lorne, heir to the Duke of Argyll, again a source of anxiety to the Queen since he was a 'commoner'. Princess Louise had many connections with the Pre-Raphaelite Brotherhood, who became friends of the Morse's.

His father, Sydney Morse was a very successful solicitor, and on 5 August 1879 joined the firm of Gedge, Kirby, Millett and Morse, 5 Lime Street Square, EC, specializing in Maritime law. His firm was associated with many institutions involved with new technologies, including tramways and electric lighting companies. He later took over the firm making it Sydney Morse & Co of Aldgate, a respected firm of family solicitors, which we used all our lives for all our legal business. He was a solid dependable fellow who gave his children great security and stability, a quality that I think Anthony inherited from him. You could say that he was representative of his time, a typical example of the ambitious professional making his way into the changing society of Victorian England.'

My grandmother's view of her father-in-law was not very well informed and not a little snobbish. She liked the royal connection and the artist in her found the art interesting. Her attitude made me reflect on how we tend to judge people by many subjective criteria, and attribute to them roles that make up only part of the individual. In her case, she did not know the family very well and Sydney Morse was her prospective father-in-law. I do not where she got this snobbish attitude from, but later in life she had a great interest in her family tree and her connection with the aristocracy. She obviously felt her own family was more aristocratic than the Morses; an opinion that grew once she had got over the first flush of romance with Anthony.

She was right in saying Sydney Morse was representative of his time. In fact, the Morse family were, although they had no aristocratic pretensions, in many ways much more remarkable than her own, who were, basically, impoverished gentry. Young Sydney Morse knew no boundaries and was not repressed by the social mores of the time. The Victorian's generally were terribly stuffy on domestic and moral questions, but the era was also one of great social change, confidence and expansion. They were Empire builders and inventors who believed the world was theirs for the taking. Sydney Morse was an example of 'the new man' emerging out of the Victorian era. He had grown up as one of twelve children, and probably, very early on in life decided he was going get on in the world and make money. He was well educated and clever. His father, Canon Francis Morse, was a poor but obviously highly intelligent parson who, after studying at Cambridge, became vicar of St Mary's Nottingham and sometimes preached in Westminster Abbey and St Paul's Cathedral; some of his sermons were published by Macmillan. He was a firm believer in education as a liberating force for the less privileged, especially women, and was amongst the founders of Nottingham High School for Girls, where two of Sydney's sisters were scholars. He sent Sydney and his brother Edward to be educated at Marlborough College, where they both played rugby for the Marlborough Nomads. As a law student in 1873-5, Sydney went on to play for England for The Law Club team against Scotland. He was described as *"a dashing runner with a good drop with either foot."* This was something my son discovered when he started to take an interest in him and it showed me, with the hindsight of three generations, that he was a much more interesting character than my grandmother portrayed in her memoirs.

Once he was able, he spent money on the things he enjoyed. Like his father, he took an active interest in education, and one of his charitable activities was to serve as joint solicitor for the School Board of London from 1890 until 1895.

> *'Sydney Morse took every opportunity to invest in works of art and the modern inventions that fascinated him, like the new American gramophone that he was reputed to have demonstrated to Queen Victoria one day, when Juliet was visiting Princess Louise at Balmoral. Paintings were his other great love and he and Juliet invested in many pictures bought from their friends.'*

My grandmother does not mention Juliet's character at all, only her connection with Princess Louise, which was how the Morses knew the Pre-Raphaelite set and Whistler. She goes on to tell the story of their dealings with Whistler:

> *'One was the American painter, James McNeill Whistler. There remain several letters and stories about Sydney Morse's relationship with Whistler, in the early days of his marriage to Juliet, when they bought Whistler's house in Cheyne Walk in Chelsea. They married in June 1878 and Whistler was invited to the wedding, after which they planned to move into his house. It appealed to them because at a time when people were wavering between heavy Victorian vulgarity*

*and the medieval opulence of William Morris, it was refreshingly simple. Whistler was a flamboyant character with a large circle of friends that included Dante Gabrielle Rosetti and Oscar Wilde. He would hold 'open house' inviting his friends over for late American breakfasts and buckwheat pancakes – all considered very racy in those days. Although Whistler was as usual very hard up, the Morses had to struggle to get him to move out of the house. He was in the middle of a court case against the great painter and art critic, John Ruskin, who had denounced Whistler's 'Nocturne in Black and Gold' saying in a review that he had 'flung a pot of paint in the public's face'. Whistler revelled in controversy and publicity. He regarded the whole business as 'a lark' and retaliated by suing Ruskin. He won the case, but with no financial benefit to himself. Instead of the **£1,000** damages he was hoping for, he was awarded a mere farthing and had to pay the costs of the case! He was by then so in debt he was not able to move into his new studio in Tite Street. Newly married, the Morses had to wait almost two months to move into their new home, in spite of buying a Chinese cabinet from him to help him out financially and hurry him along.'*

That Chinese Cabinet, with its many little drawers, was something my mother inherited. It took pride of place in the sitting room of our Percy Street flat. It hid all sorts of secret papers including a photograph of the man who was possibly my father. From time to time, when I was interested to discover my origins, I secretly took it out and compared it to my own features in the mirror, never with any conclusion. This quest, I may say, was encouraged by my grandmother, who by her questions stimulated a disapproval and fascination as to who was my mysterious, unaccounted-for father; and added to my feeling that I was quite crippled by my dysfunctional family. But back to Whistler – the artist in my grandmother was fascinated by the connection with the famous painter.

> *'The house was Whistler's labour of love; he had hand-painted most of the rooms and found it hard to let it go. Although the Morses admired the house, it was a little too flamboyant for Mrs Morse's more sober Quaker taste and they wanted to redecorate some of it. The blue and white entrance hall was painted with two ships in full sail at sea; the studio upstairs, where Whistler had done many of his paintings of the river Thames, was a sombre grey and black; the dining room flesh coloured pink with pale yellow and white on the doors. Some of the walls were painted with purple Japanese fans – Whistler was one of the first artists in England to admire and take inspiration from Japanese and Chinese art. The house was coloured as 'a sunset' with the gold dado on the stairs dotted with pink and white chrysanthemum petals. Whistler was so nervous they would ruin his beloved house that he offered to redecorate it for them. Mrs Morse later told me that he personally superintended the work and mixed the colours himself, but then a whole 'wash' for the dining room wall was spoilt as he forgot to stir it up at the right moment, causing another delay. Then they had had a great discussion about gold size. In the end, they waited*

until Whistler had gone in September before they papered over the drawing room and studio, in order to spare his feelings. Once they finally began to live there things did not go smoothly either. They had an argument with him about the latchkey to the front door. Whistler had failed to return it, and seemed to think he had the right to let himself and his servant into the house, whenever he felt like it. Sydney Morse had to send him a few stern 'solicitors letters' and withhold the final payment for the Chinese bureau, to make sure that Whistler's bohemian ideas of 'open house' did not disturb his wife in her new home. In spite of all this, they enjoyed his company and became friends with many interesting people through him and that house; Thomas Carlyle was one, the Rossettis, and Whistler's young American friend, John Singer Sargent, among others.

By the time Anthony was born it was the end of Queen Victoria's long reign, and the family had moved to Campden Hill. John Anthony Vere, as he was christened, was the last of their four children; his eldest brother was already fourteen by the time he was born. Curiously, with no idea of what the future held, I visited the house as a schoolgirl. Anthony's older sister, Enid, who was in the class above me at school, invited me for tea. I was rather proud to be asked to the home of someone higher up in the school and some years older than myself, and filled with wonder at the huge house in Airlie Gardens. Still more awe-inspiring was the austere parlour maid who opened the door, tall and dignified in a black dress with a stiff, high, white collar; and on her severe head, a little muslin cap with long white streamers hanging down behind. It is odd to think that some twenty years later she looked just the same, and that for some unexplained reason my children, Jane and Clyde, referred to her as 'Mrs 'Beefsteak and Onions'. It was a name of endearment, as although in awe of her, they appreciated her sterling qualities.

The house was a picture gallery. Paintings fitted in like a jigsaw puzzle in every room, and even covered the walls as we panted up the huge staircase to Enid's own rooms, high up in this lofty house. Pre-Raphaelite pictures mingled with Blakes and Turners, Rowlandsons and Caldecotts; they even overflowed into the lavatories and the bathroom (there was only one, goodness knows how the staff ever got a bath). John Singer Sargent's portraits of Enid and her mother found their place among them, and a drawing by Holman Hunt of Sydney Morse. I found it very difficult to digest so varied and many pictures all at once. Years later I had ample opportunity to appreciate them more fully, when I married Enid's youngest brother, Anthony.'

I remembered my own visits to Enid when we were growing up in the 1950's. We viewed her as a rather eccentric, and to our eyes rich, spinster. When she was young, she was a Pre-Raphaelite beauty who had many artist friends. The main point of interest to me as a child, in that house full of treasures, was a little musical box that had a feathered bird that flapped its wings and twittered when it was wound up and opened. I also recollect the house being full of paintings and treasures, many of which later 'disappeared' mysteriously, at the hand of a rather drunken manservant who took care of Enid in her old age. But many were sold to various museums and galleries all over the world except for a few favourites. We had two William Blake prints hanging in our nursery in the flat in Percy Street. One terrified me, as it was a strange creature running from a fire, the other was more soothing, although I never really took to it, of two guardian angels at the head and foot of a sleeping, or dead body. I was never quite sure which, hoping it was sleeping rather than dead. At some time or another during our childhood my mother sold them. They probably contributed to buying the ponies we appreciated much more than paintings. They were not really to my mother's taste either – by that time she was painting in the style of Cezanne.

Chapter 4

Anthony

1904

"The security of a mighty nation"

When the new King Edward VII (Bertie) succeeded to the throne in 1901, times moved on and entered a jollier, and more modern period than the stiff rather prudish Victorian era. For his brief reign, King Edward VII, after sowing his wild oats for many years, proved to be an immensely popular, successful king and ambassador for England.

Admiral Jack Fisher, known as 'Radical Jack Fisher', became First Sea Lord in 1904, and the Navy underwent dramatic modernization. Fisher revolutionized the design of ships, moving from the age of sail to steam, something that the old guard regarded with horror. He also pioneered the torpedo. His motto was "If you want peace, prepare for war." Lord Hankey, who served under Fisher, said of him: *'it is difficult for anyone who had not lived under the previous regime to realize what a change Fisher brought about... Before his arrival, the topics and arguments of the officers messes... were mainly confined to such matters as the cleaning of paint and brasswork... these were forgotten and replaced by incessant controversies on tactics, strategy, gunnery, torpedo warfare, blockade, etc. It was a veritable renaissance and affected every officer in the navy'.* Admiral Fisher was the driving force behind the development of the fast, all-big-gun battleships, and chaired the Committee on Designs that produced the first modern battleship, *HMS Dreadnought*, completed in 1905. After her came *HMS Invincible*, a new type of high-speed battle cruiser.

Although Britain still ruled the waves, modern technology demanded a new system of naval officer training. The Royal Naval Academy at Portsmouth had closed down in 1837 and since then new cadets trained on old wooden hulks like *HMS Britannia* on the River Dart. As early as 1875, mutterings had been made about switching naval training onshore, after concern was expressed about the health of the cadets – not to mention the standard of some of the training. Tucked into my grandmother's diary was a yellowing dog-eared letter addressed to Sydney Morse. The rather quaint letter is an insight into how the officer training must have been in those far-off days:

H.M.S Minotaur

"Dear Mr Morse,

In order to give you an idea of what your son will be doing in the next few months I send you the following description:

The instructional staff of the ship is a large one, but notwithstanding this fact, when the ship is full with 800 boys, as is sometimes the case, and especially in the winter months when the brigs and sloops attached to the ship are lying up at their ports refitting, the inadequacy of the staff is distinctly felt. However, this happily is not often the case, the standard number of boys on board averaging 600.

The instructional part of the training devolves on two lieutenants, eight warrant officers, twenty petty officer instructors, and a gunnery commander in charge of the ship. The boys have little leisure between the hours of reveille at 4.50am and the pipe 'stand by hammocks' at 8pm, but plenty of honest hard work appears to agree with 'sailor boys,' at least, judging by his healthy complexion and well set-up physique, and there is but scanty opportunity of getting into mischief, a thing most boys are apt to do if allowed much time to themselves.

The usual daily routine is as follows: After lashing up their hammocks and cleaning themselves, the boys are employed on the decks until six o'clock, when they have their breakfast which consists of four ounces of corned pork, eight ounces of soft bread, three-quarters of an ounce of chocolate, and three-quarters of an ounce of sugar. They then finish off the decks, thoroughly cleaning all the wood and bright work, and at 7.20 the 'assembly' is sounded and the boys 'told off' to man the many ship's cutters which are lowered, and pulling instruction is carried out under the second lieutenant. At eight o'clock the boats return to the ships and are hoisted up, two boats being hoisted at the same time, the band meanwhile playing the 'double' which allows the boys to run up to the 'davit head' smartly.

The range parties proceed to land, taking with them their dinners, which are cooked on shore. The classes left on board for instruction sweep up the decks for the divisional muster, which takes place at 8.45, followed by prayers read by the ship's chaplain. Prayers over, the 'instructions' bugle is sounded, classes fall in and away they go to their instructions until 3.30pm, one hour being allowed for dinner at noon. The range parties then return and instructions cease on board. The fire drill is carried out during which the lieutenant of the day visits the various stations to see everything is correct and in working order. Then 'disperse' is sounded and the boys go to supper.

Clothes have now to be washed and hung upon the clothes-lines to dry, the wet deck dried up, and everything got ready for lowering the boats. These then go away under sail, with the lieutenant on duty in the sailing pinnace, and sailing instruction is carried out until seven o'clock, when the boats' recall is hoisted and the boats return back to the ship and are hoisted up, ropes coiled down neatly, and the boys prepare their dinners for the next day.

Now it is very nearly time to 'stand by hammocks', and willingly the boys turn in and soon go to sleep after their hard day's work in the fresh sea air - indeed, so much so, that when the first lieutenant goes his rounds at nine o'clock he finds the decks quiet and peaceful. Here and there, dotted around, are the nice clean white hammocks; and inside them, if one takes a peep, one sees a little sleeping form, snugly tucked between the blankets, as often as not snoring like a young steam engine. What a change from the activity of a couple of hours ago!

On Thursday's and Sunday's the boys have 'plum duff' with their dinners, and on these auspicious days they are allowed afternoon leave on shore. Whilst writing the words 'plum duff' an amusing incident runs through my mind. The other day I was inspecting the boy's dinners. It was a Thursday, and on arriving at the band-boys' mess I noticed that there were no currants or raisins in the pudding; in fact, the 'duff' was deserted in this respect. I questioned a cook-of-the-mess – a boy of about 4-ft nothing in height, with little beam and enormous eyes, in fact, he was nearly all eyes. As to the reason – the boy blushingly stammered out that when making the pudding the evening before he had not the strength of mind to resist eating the raisins, as 'they looked so nice'. The boy was not allowed to be cook-of-the-mess in the future.

Wednesday forenoon is a great day in the week. The battalion is landed and drawn up on shore by eight o'clock, and then, with band playing and flags flying the boys are marched up to the parade ground where battalion and company drill is exercised. Once a year an inter-training-ship boat race comes off for a challenge cup subscribed for between all the ships. The contest takes place at a different port each year in order to give crews from each ship in turn a chance of pulling on their own particular water. The several crews arrive some days previous to the race, and it is the event that creates the greatest excitement of the year. The *Minotaur* won the race both last year and in 1901, and she is the first ship to have won the race two years in succession, proving that although much time is devoted to gunnery on board her, boat pulling is in no wise allowed to deteriorate.

And with this brief account - brief solely by reason of little space, as much more might be said upon the matter - I am reluctantly obliged to take my leave, in the sincere hope you may appreciate in its true value the life on board a training-ship, watching with interest the gradual piecing together of that living belt of defence that has grown year by year and bolt by bolt into the saving strength and security of a mighty nation."

Warrant Officer P.B. Elliott

I thought of young men today and wondered how they would fare under this discipline. My grandfather started his life in the Navy on a similar ship, but only for a few months. Before Fisher's time, the recruitment of naval officers, as with the army, had been largely amongst the younger sons of aristocrats, who could afford to buy themselves a commission. Fisher, a middle-class, workaholic believed passionately that *'an exclusive system of nomination is distasteful, if not alien, to the democratic sentiment.'* He designed a new *'common entrance scheme that every fit boy should have his chance, irrespective of the depth of his parents' purse'*. Entrance by examination only, which previously biased the intake to those who could obtain special tuition, was replaced with an interview committee, which determined the general knowledge of candidates, judging their reaction to the questions as much as their answers. The standard was very high. Training was extended from two years to four, resulting in a need for more accommodation for cadets.

When he was twelve, my grandfather went into the Navy. He wrote the following letter home to his mother:

Admiralty House
Portsmouth

Aug 13 1904

Dear Mother

I hope you are quite well. I am not staying at the Pier Hotel but at Sir John Fisher's house, he himself is here tonight, there is going to be a big dinner party, as there is no place for me I am not going to have to have dinner with the others (much to my joy) but alone. I had a very nice journey and when I arrived at your sister I met Sir Henry just *going to Sir John Fisher's so we went off together after dinner. I went all over the docks, and we were on the Victory an hour-and-a-half. The rest of the time we spent going about the harbour. It was awful fun on the Victory. Our proper boat, which we were going in with two other boys, the two boys had bagged and gone off in and we could not find them, and so that (I) was left alone. We are going for a trip tomorrow, where I do not know. It is a lovely house in which I am staying. There is another admiral here whom I like very much, he took me all round the docks and showed me everything.*

Best love

Ant

It was 100 years after Admiral Lord Nelson's victory at Trafalgar. In those days the Navy was still a way of life rather than a career. It was not until after World War II and he retired in 1946, as a Vice Admiral, that my grandfather ventured to do anything other than serve his king and country. He spent a short time at Osborne on the Isle of Wight. The Osborne Naval College was in Queen Victoria's beloved home, which had been donated to the nation. It was by all accounts, also, very tough. Jack Llewellyn Davis, my grandfather's future friend, complained bitterly about it.

He was destined for Dartmouth, the impressive naval officer training college that was just being completed, designed by Sir Aston Webb, the architect of the façade of Buckingham Palace. It was huge, could accommodate far more cadets, and was a modern advance from the old system on board a training ship. Sydney Morse had enrolled his son at the new college. He would spend four years there before graduating and going on board ship at the age of 17. The conditions were probably less spartan than the training ship, but discipline in the new college was strict and study intense. Cadets received an education in science and technology, as it related to life onboard a ship, as well as the normal naval exercises of sailing and navigation with use of a chart and compass. Those who went on to be command officers would have the benefit of understanding their ships, while those who became engineers would be better equipped for command. There was mathematics, pure and high theoretical, spherical trigonometry, algebra, physics, chemistry, nautical astronomy, naval history, English and French. The work was examined several times a year. Physical education and sport were taught, not only for the benefit of the cadets, but also for the future training of ships crews, who were expected to produce sporting teams on goodwill visits in foreign ports. After four years, cadets were posted to special training ships for final practical experience before being given real command positions. The results of the final examination affected the seniority allotted to each cadet and his chance of future early promotion.

Chapter 5

Marly

1914

Bum Boating

My grandmother continued with her story:

'That summer, while sitting on the cliffs to the east of Warbarrow Bay in Dorset making a sketch of the cliff and the sea beyond, I was given the opportunity to add greatly to the interest of my picture. The magnificent sight of a fleet of battleships appeared before me steaming to the east. I realized it was a curious sight for those waters in early August, and by the next day I knew only too well why I had seen them there. It was the Grand Fleet making their way to Scapa Flow. Britain was preparing for War.

The fleet had been ordered to sail from Portland for its war station at Scapa Flow, in the most northerly Orkney Isles. This position commanded the North Sea and they would be in instant readiness for action if the enemy appeared. Throughout the war they would operate from there, keeping up the pressure on the German fleet. At that moment I could not help but be impressed by the sight. What I did not grasp at the time was that the show of strength presaged a war more horrible than ever so far in our history. Most of us thought it would be a professional war with the Navy defending our island, as she had always done in the Napoleonic, Dutch and Spanish wars of the past, and it would be over by Christmas. As an island, we thought it would be fought on the Continent as usual and would not affect us greatly. We did not realize it would involve the whole country and, instead of direct confrontation with the enemy and the more old fashioned head on battle, an unprecedented type of conflict would be used, where the enemy could be outgunned at a distance and speed was of the essence.

Unknown to me, one of those ships in the fleet heading for Scapa Flow in August 1914 was carrying Anthony, but it was at least a year before I was to meet him. He spent a brief period of waiting and training in Scapa Flow, in a seemingly endless and tedious hide-and-seek with the German Fleet in the North Sea, until he was sent to more distant battlefields.

Once I knew what the sight meant I hurried to the Bembridge, where I felt safe and at home. I still loved the life there and the added bonus was that the Sailing Club, along with the Garland and Royal Yacht Squadron, was extremely fashionable and gay. A war seemed very far away, but I had an underlying feeling that I should make a contribution. At first I was at a loss as to what I could do, but one day at the Sailing Club I met 'Uncle' Ricardo, a sailor who had run away from Eton and gone to sea 'before the mast', and was operating a 'Bum-boat'. I realized that from my long association with the Thornycroft family I was fairly handy about a boat. I decided to persuade him to take me on as his 'crew', even though he was at first very wary of having a woman on board. In the end, I convinced him that he would not be let down or embarrassed by me, and after a trial run, he finally agreed. I had no idea then how momentous the decision was for me. It started me off on a new phase in life that eventually led to my marriage.

Everyday we chugged out of Bembridge harbour from Spithead, in the little motorboat "Catapult", to meet the ships and minesweepers out in the Solent. Our cargo was 'fags' and newspapers, kippers, a large churn of milk and fresh eggs, green vegetables and apples. We took stamps, collected letters and fulfilled any other requests from the sailors. I thoroughly enjoyed the job. The Spithead gradually became the anchorage for more and more craft of all kinds. Some days there were so many ships that we had to go back to harbour several times to reload, in order to cope with their many requests.

The first Destroyer that ever visited was a pleasant surprise for us. As we came alongside HMS Harpy, we were peremptorily told to go up for'ard, and, of course, we obeyed. The sailors, who had been at sea without returning to harbour for many days and nights seemed overjoyed to see us, keeping us hectically busy asking for things.

Marly and 'Uncle Ricardo' on the *Catapult*

Out of the corner of my eye I could see the Captain from the bridge having a good look at us through his binoculars. Soon a very polite message was sent asking if we would be so kind as to come aft before we left. The Captain, I soon found out, was Gerald Charles Dickens, grandson of the famous writer Charles.

Captain Gerald Dickens

His sub-Lieutenant was Jack Llewellyn Davies, whose mother Sylvia du Maurier was a friend of James Barrie, the creator of 'Peter Pan'. Quite a literary command! I discovered later, although he was very reluctant to admit it, Jack was one of the children who had been the inspiration for the story. So here was something quite different from the usual customers, and for the Captain and Lieutenant, I was an interesting change from the normal 'Bum-boat' personnel.

"Come along into my cabin," said Commander Dickens. "This is a grand job you are doing, and we must celebrate our first meeting". "Where's that young Sub of mine?" he muttered. "If the 'crew' isn't one for drinks we must produce something else."

Jack then appeared with a large box of Charbonnel and Walker chocolates. "Just arrived by the mail," he said. "Please have them."

I was very excited by the meeting and found Jack very handsome. I thought him extremely charming and even better looking than his uncle, Gerald du Maurier, the actor whom I had greatly admired as a girl. I noticed on the desk of Commander Dickens, 'Dick', as we soon called him, fascinating illustrations of his thoughts scribbled on blotting paper, charts, naval signals or any other handy stationery provided by the Admiralty. In my fanciful way, I imagined that if he had not been a sailor he could have made his name as a writer, and, illustrated his own books; that he had the same wide human sympathy and insight into character as his illustrious grandfather. We all got on like a house on fire. They soon persuaded us that the ship was our second home and we need only say the word, and anything that His Majesty's destroyer Harpy could do for us, she would.

During that winter I found that the job I had started so joyfully in August became much more difficult. The cold winds and rough seas gave me a facial paralysis that I finally discovered had the name of

'Bell's Disease', and I decided I ought to look for a job in a hospital in London. I tried it for a while but was not good at it at all and so the following spring returned to the 'Bum-boat'. On the next trip out to The Harpy, Jack invited me to meet him in London on his next leave. I was terribly pleased and rushed up to London to 'Woollands' and bought a new hat and dress. He had reserved a table for luncheon at the Savoy and a magnum of champagne.

Somehow the lunch was not what I had romantically expected it to be. Jack and I did not seem so much in tune as when I was tossing about on the sea, clad in an oily and sou'wester. He obviously decided I was not the one for him and I was a little disappointed, ruefully thinking perhaps it was the hat, or my dress. We spent the afternoon together, however, and talked on into the evening about life and marriage. Although Jack did not turn out to be the man I was destined to marry, I did find in him a kindred spirit to whom I could talk about the things I hoped for and loved.

Finally, he said to me in a very fatherly manner: "Therefore, my dear girl, it's perfectly obvious that you must marry a sailor."

I returned happily to my work on the Bum Boat, not taking too much notice of Jack Llewellyn's remarks about marrying a sailor. 'Uncle' had taken a rather dim view of the whole escapade as he had come to depend on me. Jack, however, obviously had not forgotten. The next time we boarded HMS Harpy, I found myself faced with almost an ultimatum.

"A really marvellous chap, who once served with both of us, is now on leave. You must go up to London with Jack who will take you to meet him." Dick said.

"I don't feel that he could be any more marvellous than the people I already have the opportunity of meeting every day." I said, but was soon made to feel small by Dick.

"My dear Crew, you don't know what you are talking about. Here's a fellow who took part in the landing at the Dardanelles, and although only a Sub–Lieutenant, showed such conspicuous bravery that he was awarded the DSO – one of the first in this war. The Prime Minister, Asquith, described it as 'quite one of the romantic episodes of the War'.

I thought to myself that although women are said to be inveterate matchmakers, nothing could compare with men for perseverance and organization of the matter once they got down to it.'

Chapter 6

Anthony 1915

The Dardanelles – Before the battle

My grandfather, after a short time in Scapa Flow, probably on one of the ships my grandmother had seen, was sent out as part of the fleet sent to knock the Ottoman Empire out of the War, and keep Allied supply lines clear through the Mediterranean. He was freshly qualified from Dartmouth, on board the *HMS Nubian*, one of Jack Fisher's Tribal Class destroyers. She burnt diesel fuel, instead of the old fashioned coal that had meant constant refuelling in port. The flagship, *Queen Elizabeth*, was the most powerful warship afloat, boasting 15-inch guns. She was leading 18 Allied battleships with supporting cruisers and destroyers. It was an impressive array of British might and power and he, like many young men from all over the Empire, were confidently looking forward to their first battle, beating back the Turk and German.

My grandfather as a young lieutenant

The Dardanelles is a narrow stretch of water leading from the Aegean to the Sea of Marmara, which in turn leads to Constantinople and on to the Black Sea, through the Bosphorus. Now I wished I had known my grandfather's history when I travelled to Istanbul in the 1970's, but in those days I would not have appreciated it.

In the months leading up to the War, Asquith's government was plunged into a crisis in this area. In January 1914 Tzar Nicholas of Russia appealed to Lord Kitchener, the Governor of Egypt, to help them open up the Dardanelles. Kitchener was reluctant to get involved and hesitant to alienate Muslims, who formed a large part of the British

Empire and supplied thousands of troops. He was even less inclined when war was declared with Germany and he became Secretary of State for War; the losses on the Western Front left him with few to spare.

Historically, England had always protected the Ottoman Khalifate; its geographical position was critical to the preservation of the British Empire. Asquith's Liberal government, however, regarded Turkey as the 'Sick Man of Europe', an opinion largely based on Winston Churchill's earlier reports that the Khalifate was 'scandalous, decrepit and no longer with any influence'. In 1909 Enver Pasha and his Young Turks (a group of western educated liberal secularists) had overthrown the last true Sultan Abdalhamid, and Mahmud V was put in power as a puppet Khalif. In 1911 Churchill further alienated the Turks when, as First Lord of the Admiralty, he rejected an offer of a permanent alliance.

As war broke out the Ottomans prevaricated, hoping to back the winning side. They loosely allied themselves with Austria and Germany against Britain, France and Russia. Enver Pasha and his Minister of War, Colonel Mustapha Kemal, admired and supported the Germans who had trained the Ottoman Army. The German Kaiser (one of George V's more problematic cousins) was obsessed with building an Empire to match that of England's, and had his eye on Turkey as his route to North Africa. He wanted to keep the Dardanelles firmly closed for – 'if the Russians could not export their wheat or import war materials the country would gradually collapse'. His motives were rather a matter of family rivalry going global.

The British, had trained the Turkish Navy and built their ships. Churchill (encouraged by King George V who wished to support his other cousin, the Tzar) decided that the British Government should capture Constantinople and help the Russians open up the Dardanelle straits, a vital exit into the Mediterranean.

Just before the War the British played their cards wrong. Two incidents occurred helping to push the Turks onto the side of Germany. The first was in the Tyne shipyards. The Ottomans had commissioned two new Dreadnoughts, now all the rage in every Navy in Europe. In July, during the crisis leading up to the War, *Sultan Osman* and *Reshadieh* were finally completed. The Turkish captain arrived for delivery on 2nd August, only to be told by Churchill that since Britain was now at war with Germany, she could not possibly allow enemy ships to leave her harbours; she was requisitioning the ships for her own. The Prime Minister, Sir Edward Grey, sent his 'sincere regrets' to the Turks and forbade the captain, Mr Rauf, to leave English waters. The ships were renamed *HMS Agincourt* and *Erin* and remained in the British Navy. The Turkish government was infuriated and insulted, and later it emerged, that thousands of Anatolian peasants had contributed to the cost, £7,500,000 out of their own pockets. The next day Turkey made a secret agreement with Germany.

The second incident was also just before the outbreak of the War. Two British Admirals, Sir Berkeley Milne and Sir Ernest Troubridge, were in command of a large Allied Mediterranean Fleet. Admiral John Fisher had opposed the command of Milne and favoured Admiral Limpus, who knew the area but had recently been expelled from the Turkish Naval Mission, over the affair of the *Osman* and *Reshadieh*. Kitchener, reluctant to stir up more trouble with the Turks, disagreed. There were only two German ships in the area, the *Goeben* – a large battleship of the same speed as the British battlecruisers, and *Breslau* – a light cruiser. The Allied Fleet was more than an equal match to the Germans. By a series of blunders Milne and Troubridge with three fast, modern battlecruisers *HMS Inflexible, Indefatigable* and *Indomitable*, four armoured cruisers, four light cruisers and a flotilla of 14 destroyers, managed to lose the two German battleships. What they did not realize was that the German Admiral Souchon had obtained permission from the Turks, for safe passage through the heavily mined Dardanelle Straits, and had slipped through unnoticed. When Milne eventually realized what had happened, instead of following them in and making short work of them by force of numbers, he hesitated and waited at the mouth of the Straits, expecting the Germans to come back out into the Mediterranean. The German ships meanwhile, instead of re-emerging into the Mediterranean arrived in Constantinople, causing an international uproar because Turkey (still claiming to be neutral) was bound by treaty to prevent German ships passing through the Straits. A meeting was called to discuss the embarrassing situation, and one of the ministers came up with the bright idea that would deal poetic justice to the British – that the Germans 'donate' the two battleships to Turkey, replacing the ones the British had so unreasonably seized previously. Tit for Tat! Suddenly Germany became immensely popular with the Turkish public. On 16th August, *Goeben* and *Breslau* were quickly renamed *Jawus* and *Midilli*, Turkish flags hoisted in lieu of German ones, the crew given fezzes and reviewed by the Sultan Mehmed V, amidst jubilation and parades in Constantinople. In October, the Germans decided the Turkish procrastination should come to a head, and Admiral Souchon engineered an act of war with the newly named Turkish/German ships, taking them into the Black Sea bombing Sebastopol and Odessa, and sinking a Russian gunboat. The Russians, infuriated, now firmly took the Allied side. Turkey could no longer to pretend to be neutral. On 14th November, the Shaykh-al-Islam was persuaded to declare an 'Islamic Jihad' on behalf of the Khalif, Sultan Mehmed V, against Britain, France, Russia, Serbia and Montenegro. Milne and Troubridge both lost their commands.

In spite of all this, Churchill was still enthusiastic about the idea of opening up the Dardanelles and capturing Constantinople for

Britain. It had the added benefit of occupying the Germans in another area, and taking the pressure off the Western Front, which was going disastrously. Admiral Fisher, argued against the whole idea but Churchill, although he respected Fisher, in his usual determined way, won the argument. In the end Fisher came round, but continued to insist that the Navy could not manage the campaign without the back up of Army troops.

Churchill cabled Admiral Carden, who was now in command in the Mediterranean, after the fiasco of the *Goeben* and *Breslau,* asking his advice on forcing the Straits. His reply was: 'I do not consider the Dardanelles can be rushed'. But on 19th February he was ordered to start the first bombardment of the forts on the Straits, targeting the narrowest point of the Dardanelles, just a mile wide. The ships fired their heavy guns across the peninsula, and then moved towards the Straits. There seemed little opposition, so some marines landed and destroyed the outlying guns. The fleet felt very confident and believed victory was inevitable. Their certainty was bolstered even more by a German wireless message they picked up, reporting that the Dardanelle forts were running out of ammunition. (Later, to their cost, they found out that the message was only partially true and the Ottomans had been panicking.) The mood at that point was buoyant, and Admiral Carden optimistically cabled Churchill on 4th March, saying that the fleet could expect to arrive in Constantinople within fourteen days. He ordered British minesweepers to proceed along the Straits; unfortunately the civilians who manned them did not do a proper job, as they disliked having to work under Turkish fire, and were hampered by a strong current. They left the minefields largely intact. On March 11th Carden received an impatient telegram from London, saying he should decide on a date of attack soon, and would not be held responsible for the results. Feeling pressured, he cabled back saying that their main attack would be launched on or around 17th March. In those early days of the War, wireless communication was slow and caused a lot of the confusion, and on 13th, while still waiting to hear back from London, he sent one of his ships into the Straits. She was badly damaged. On 15th he finally received the go-ahead from the Admiralty, but by that time he was suffering from such stress that the medical officer had placed him on the sick list. Admiral de Robeck, his second in command, took over with only three days to prepare, but by this time many of the crew were unsure of their command, and complaining about Whitehall's bungling. They, like Lord Fisher, were concerned that they would not be able to deal with the Turkish guns by bombardment from the ships alone.

On 18th March they launched the main attack, entering the Dardanelle straits. They did some damage to the Turkish forts and by the afternoon the return gunfire from the forts was practically silenced, with no damage to the ships. The fleet advanced further sending the minesweepers before them. All seemed well, until suddenly, as they were withdrawing through Eren Keui Bay just inside the straits, there was a tremendous explosion and a French battleship capsized with its entire crew aboard and rapidly sank. Two more British ships were damaged, although nobody was sure during the battle whether mines or torpedoes were responsible. In the evening, when most of the ships had got clear, one more rescue ship was sent in and was struck by an explosion, sinking along with the ship it had gone to rescue. They were all perplexed and badly shaken. They had lost 61 men in casualties, and out of the 18 Allied battleships, 3 had sunk and 3 more were badly damaged. Later, they found out the reason. The Ottomans in the forts had noticed on previous forays that the Allied ships turned starboard into the Eren Keui Bay as they left the Straits, so unobserved, ten days earlier, a little Ottoman steamer *Nusret* had placed a new line of mines.

Admiral de Robeck was distraught from the losses in his first command, and thought he would find himself superseded the next morning. He felt he had been responsible for the most serious loss to the Royal Navy since Trafalgar, and that sacrificing further ships was the worst thing a sailor could do. But far from being substituted, De Robeck got word from the Admiralty that they were sending five more battleships out to replace those lost. They should keep up the attack; Churchill had decided that the Navy had a large number of obsolete battleships, too old to be used in the North Sea against the Germans, but which could be put to use in this campaign.

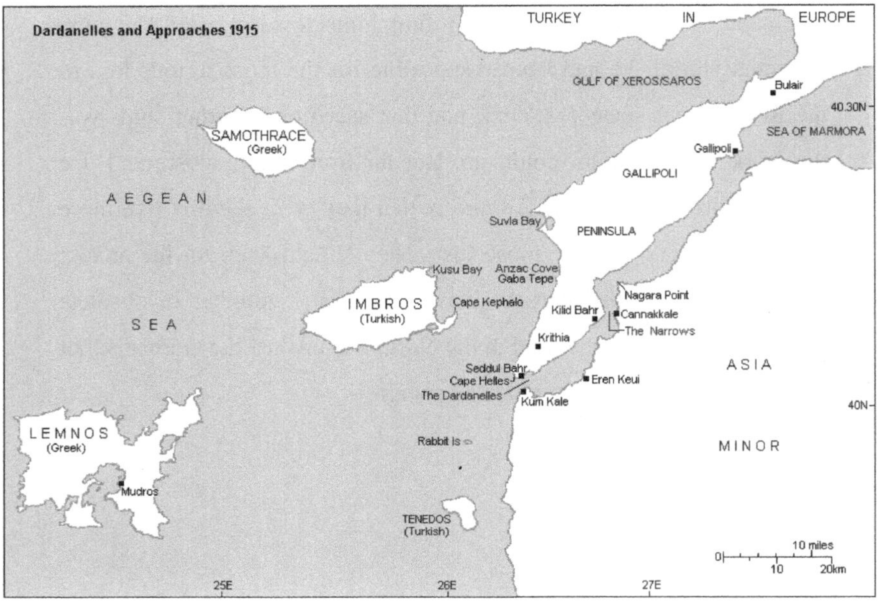

Approaches to Dardanelles www.naval-history.net

Chapter 7

The Dardanelles – The Trojan Horse

"Today's news of the Dardanelles is quite good, and illustrates the truth that in this extraordinary War all the oldest, as well as the most modern devices come in. The Trojan Horse, for instance, 2,000 soldiers who were unable to land were shut up in a collier, the decks covered with coal, & the sides made openable & flappable. And then when night came on, she was run ashore and they emerged from their cupboard & were all safely landed."
Herbert Asquith

The Fleet withdrew to the Greek island of Lemnos, their collection point and base, to lick their wounds. They used the abandoned harbour of Mudros to make repairs and prepare for the next attack. Members of the crews reported that the lovely small island, with grass, clover and wild flowers growing everywhere, was a welcome respite. It was like stepping back 100 years in time; the little scattered villages built of rough stone were still very primitive. The islanders made their own clothes, spinning raw wool from their sheep, and they still ploughed with an ancient iron hoe attached to a piece of wood. The men were dressed in clothes cut from goat and sheepskins. At first people were welcoming and helpful. There was an abundance of olives, dried grapes and figs and it could have been a paradise, if it had not quickly been converted into a living nightmare by the chaos of unprepared troops arriving from Egypt.

Lord Kitchener and the Cabinet in London, after the losses they had suffered, now agreed with Admiral Fisher on the necessity of a Combined Operation. They hurriedly sent out General Sir Ian Hamilton, to command a Mediterranean Expeditionary Force to support the Navy. He was whisked from Europe to Lemnos, in a matter of days, and arrived the day before the planned second Naval attack. London urgently ordered a lot of raw troops to Mudros, consisting largely of the Anzacs (Australian and New Zealand volunteer soldiers) who had been training in Egypt, on standby for the trenches in France. They were to form the Expeditionary Force. The men, who had volunteered full of patriotism and enthusiasm, looking forward to their first encounters, were quickly disillusioned as to what was actually happening. Battalions and their equipment had been split up between ships, and now things could not be found. The situation was about as black as black could be, and the troops were complaining that they had been told nothing but lies. My grandfather later told my grandmother that he greatly admired the Anzacs; they always had such high spirits. Like him, most of them had come straight from college, or in some cases from the outback, and it was their first experience of war. He was shocked at the chaos, but as a young Lieutenant he had little influence and could only help in small ways. General Hamilton found Mudros to be a very unsuitable harbour. There was no drinking water, shelter or piers and the March weather was extremely unfavourable for a renewed attack. So he changed his base to Alexandria, transporting many of the men back to where they had just come from, losing valuable time, and giving the Turks and Germans an opportunity to work out what was happening, re-arm and bring in more troops.

By March 22nd Admiral de Robeck had assessed the situation and he sat down with General Hamilton to try and sort out the muddle. The Navy and Army were not accustomed to working together but it was their only hope. The plan was for the Navy to land the Army on five different beaches, S, V, W, X and Y along the Cape Helles peninsula.

My grandfather was assigned to the landing on V beach, or Seddul Bahr Bay, its Turkish name. It was anticipated to be the most difficult because the coast there had the best defences. Although most of the landings were to be made from open boats, they decided in this case, the majority of the covering force should be disembarked from a tramp steamer *SS River Clyde* – originally a 4,000-ton collier built in Glasgow in 1905. She was one of the redundant ships Churchill sent for the attack. Her Commander, Edward Unwin, was a former merchant seaman and naval officer, who was also a classical scholar. Inspired by the proximity to Troy, it was his idea to use the *River Clyde* as a Trojan Horse.

At Mudros harbour the ship underwent her preparation. She was to carry 2,000 troops under camouflage into the Seddul Bahr Bay. The steel hull was painted yellow to look like sand. Eight doorways were cut out along the side, to provide sally ports just large enough for a fully equipped man to pass through; from there, gangways would lead to a bridge of flat bottom boats, or 'lighters', linking the ship to the beach. They had a job to finish it in time, but all the forces pulled together. The Royal Naval Service, commanded by Lieutenant-Commander Josiah Wedgewood, provided a battery of eleven

Gallipoli Landings and Battleship Losses 1915

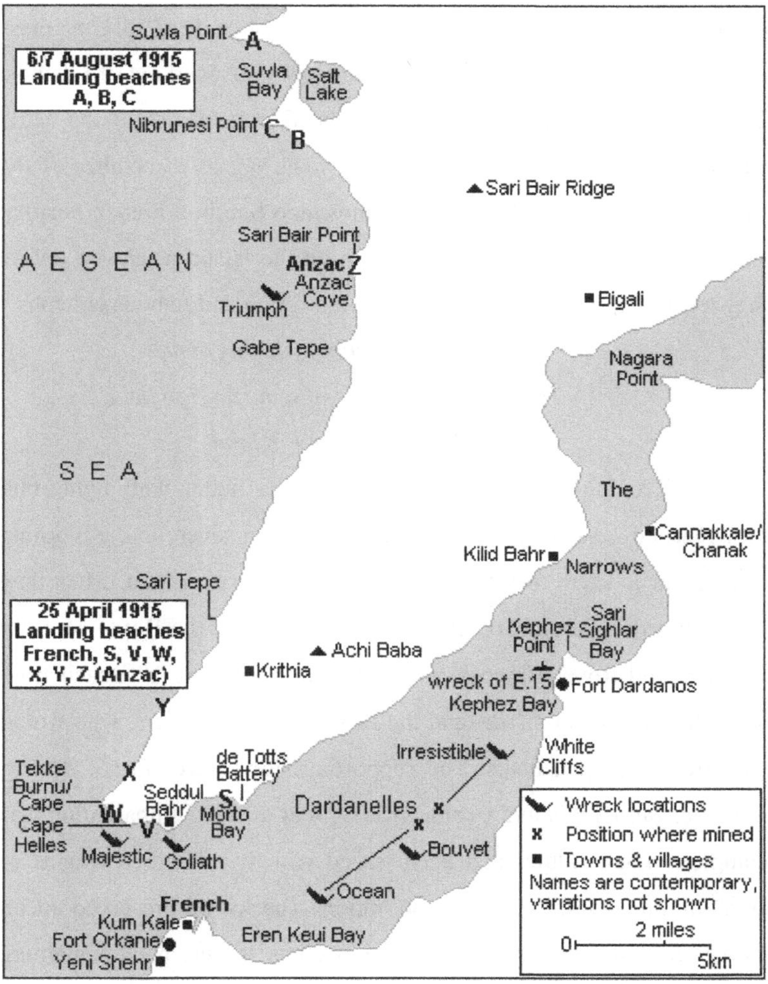

Map by Gordon Smith, please acknowledge www.naval-history.net

Maxim machine guns, which were mounted on sandbags, on the bow behind the boilerplate. Commander Unwin then asked for volunteers from his own ship as crew. He chose six seamen, six engine-room ratings, and a shipwright. A very keen young able-seaman named Williams, pushed his way forward and asked if he could go too. Unwin thought him too young and told him he did not want an able-seaman. He pleaded: 'I'll chuck my rate if only you will let me come.' Such was the enthusiasm, and I have to say, naivety but bravery, of the young combatants of the First World War. On the night of April 23rd, the mass of old ships picked up their anchors and slowly steamed out of Lemnos. That night, before they sailed, one of the first casualties of the battle was the poet Rupert Brooke, who had come out as a member of the Royal Naval Division. He died of a mosquito bite in a French hospital ship off Skyros. His friend buried him on the island at eleven before they left harbour. He had written himself a fitting and famous epitaph:

If I should die think only this of me:
That there's a corner of some foreign field
That is forever England.

Keeping the same speed through the night, with lights out, they reached Tenedos about forty miles away, at seven on the morning of 24th April. There they waited until three in the afternoon, when they received orders to embark the troops. These were, the Royal Munster Fusiliers and Royal Hampshires, who were to land at 'V' Beach from the hull of the *River Clyde*, and the Royal Dublin Fusiliers, who would land from the open boats. The supporting ships were *H.M.S. Albion, Lord Nelson, Dublin* and *Cornwallis*. By that evening embarkation was complete. Each soldier had been issued with two hundred rounds of ammunition and three days iron rations (packs of preserved meat, cheese, biscuit, tea, sugar and salt), as well as another pack containing their greatcoats and waterproof sheets (for many, these proved to be a fatal load). At one in the morning on 25th April, the *Clyde* and the other ships slowly started to steam towards their objective. They were all excited about the battle and that night the troops were as happy as they could possibly be, especially the Australian and New Zealanders, mandolins, guitars and banjos going for all they were worth. Nobody thought of what was going to happen on the morrow. The soldiers bedded down about 10 o'clock with everything ready for an instant move. Hot cocoa was to be issued just before dawn.

As the sun started to come up over the Aegean sea, General Sir Ian Hamilton watching the operation from the flagship *HMS Queen Elizabeth* prayed: "Almighty God, Watchman of the Milky Way, Shepherd of the Golden Stars, have mercy upon us ... Thy will be done. *En avant* — at all costs — *en avant*."

At five the *River Clyde* steamed slowly into Seddul-Bahr Bay. The day was a lovely and clear, but the sun rising in their faces made it very difficult for them to see the shore. As they approached, the Turkish defences started bombarding them from trenches perched on the cliffs. The perpendicular cliffs to the west formed a natural amphitheatre; to the east was the old castle and village of Seddul-Bahr.The rifle and machine-gun rattle was incessant and smoke from the bursting shells made it doubly difficult to see. They were like sitting ducks! All troops were ordered to stay below deck. The ship headed up to the beach and was run ashore at about half-past six and grounded without the slightest jar. The plan had been that the soldiers would reach the beach under the shelter of the ship's camouflaged plating, and pass over a bridge of barges forming a gangway right up to the shore. But although Commander Unwin put the *River Clyde* ashore exactly as planned, they had not reckoned on the force of the strong current, so instead of going straight ahead as expected, the steamer hopper towing the lighters sheered off to port. The towrope could not be cleared and the *Clyde* failed to go ahead as intended. The shore there was steep, the gap too large for the men to cross and the water out of a man's depth. Midshipman Drewry, in charge of the hopper, started to hack away with an axe trying to cut the towrope. Unwin dashed over to the port side of the ship, realizing that if it was not cleared, they would not be able to get the lighters into position in time to be of use. He climbed down over the starboard bow on to the lighters, which had also shot ahead, pulled by the hopper. My grandfather, with Midshipman Malleson from the *Cornwallis*, came to help grabbing the line and giving it to Unwin, who swam ashore. Unwin, assisted by the young volunteer able-seaman Williams, who had followed him, hauled the lighters towards him. They were standing up to their shoulders in water, fully exposed to the rifle and machine-gun fire of the Turkish troops from the hills, and from their own warships blazing away from further out at sea behind the *Clyde*. Finally, they got the lighters into position with the beach and called the troops to disembark. The soldiers bravely responded, but as they dashed for the shore across the gangways, they were picked off by tornados of shot and shell, and only 20 of 200 reached the shore alive. When one of the lighters broke away and drifted into deep water with the soldiers on it, some men jumped over the side in an endeavour to make the shore, but many sank owing to the weight of their equipment (all those rations) and were drowned.

General Sir Ian Hamilton, watching from the *Queen Elizabeth* through his glass, could see the sea being whipped up all along the beach and around the *River Clyde,* by a pelting storm of rifle bullets; the brave troops up to their necks in the tormented water trying to struggle on to land.

SS Clyde with Turkish Shells exploding in Seddul-Bahr
© IWM (Q 13697)

I can only imagine, with the help of films like 'Gallipoli' and descriptions from the war records, what the intensity of such a battle would have been like for my grandfather and his companions. It must have been quite overwhelming, but as in any extreme situation they concentrated on the work in front of them. He and his fellows were highly trained, strictly disciplined and they did their duty. Commander Unwin and young Williams, still holding onto the line, were by now standing in a sea of blood. After about forty minutes of this, Williams gave a gasp, saying a shell had struck him and fell into Unwin's arms. Unwin had to hold him up in case he should fall and drown, and in doing so was forced to let go of the rope. The offshore wind made the lighters start to drift away just as my grandfather and two others, who had been working around the hopper came back on the scene. They spent some hours up to their waists in water under heavy fire, helping to hold together the broken bridge of lighters. Commander Unwin, who by that time was suffering extreme exhaustion, dragged young Williams to a place of comparative safety, and then, he himself had to be taken back to the *River Clyde* for medical treatment. Williams, however, had succumbed to his injuries. Unwin later regretted allowing him to come saying: 'I shall never forget the way he died.'

Midshipmen Drewry and Malleson, helped by an engineer, set to work to restore the broken line of lighters with enough success to enable Drewry, as he was carried below with a bullet wound on the forehead, to report to Commander Unwin: 'I have made the connection, Sir.'

Unwin was at that moment coming out of his cabin, where for an hour the doctors had been trying to get his heart to work normally. As soon as he was able, he went down again into the hopper to try and improve the connection, helped by an old merchant seaman of about 70 and a boy under 18, who both faced the fire without hesitation. They had to give up when Unwin was wounded by bullet splinters in the face, and was forced to return to the ship for further medical treatment. About noon, my grandfather went aboard the *Queen Elizabeth* requesting ammunition for the naval machine-guns. He described to Commodore Roger Keyes the desperate fighting and severe losses. Keyes said: "We were all struck by the bearing of Morse during the recital of his tale, and when he left us to return to the inferno round the *River Clyde*, I must confess I never expected to see him again." All day the *River Clyde* was under heavy fire from the Ottomans, and by evening in spite of all their efforts, a thousand troops were still on board waiting to disembark when darkness fell.

By one in the morning on 26th April, twenty-four hours since they had started their attack, the troops landed successfully under cover of darkness and established their positions. The *Albion*, one of the ships covering the landing, sent in her launch manned by volunteers to help form the bridge. Their crews helped to get the wounded from the beach and the lighters back into the *River Clyde.* Everyone was beyond exhaustion and although they had had nothing to eat or drink for 48 hours, except for that cup of chocolate before the battle, curiously none of them felt the want of food or drink. They got a very welcome cup of tea in the trawler that night.

For most of them it was the first time they had witnessed their friends and shipmates dying in front of them. They kept on through the night never stopping until they had got all the wounded back to the *Clyde* for treatment. One of the doctors had been shot in the foot but, although in great pain, he carried on treating people until the next day. Midshipman Drewry afterwards said: 'I never knew blood smelt so strong before'.

The whole battle is faithfully reported in detail by many of the participants and, of course, in the Royal Navy records. There were many stories of great courage and endurance on both sides. The Allies knew the Turks did not like bayonets, which they used for counter-attacks and successfully drove off many, but they found that the Turks had been reinforced overnight. Early that morning, the crew of the *River Clyde* could see the Turks creeping along the hilltops, trying to get closer and shooting repeatedly, in order to drive the Allied soldiers from their position on the beach. The seven warships edged into the bay, with the *Queen Elizabeth* behind as a kind of chaperone. Each warship covered a section, bombarding the heights and valley beyond with every kind of shell they had – from the *Queen Elizabeth's* 18-inch shrapnel to 12-pounders. The shooting was excellent, but the Ottomans had splendid cover, so they kept advancing and trying to drive off the ships with their guns. In the end the Turkish defenders proved too few to force them off the beach, although they defended every inch of their soil furiously, and the Allies acknowledged their bravery.

By the evening they heard that Cape Helles had been taken, beaches X, W and V were secure in Allied hands. They had to leave *River Clyde* where she was beached, and gradually the supporting ships rescued and transported the wounded back to Lemnos to recuperate. There they heard about the many losses on the other beaches, except for Y where the landings had been relatively easy.

The Allies kept up the attacks until May, when the *Queen Elizabeth* was sent home. She was too precious to risk submarine and torpedo attacks. In August, the Turks took back Sulva, and it seemed the whole campaign had been in vain. Suvla became known as Anzac Cove, in memory of so many young Australians and New Zealanders who lost their lives there. Trench warfare continued but as it got hotter it became more difficult, and there were terrible problems with dysentery breaking out. The medical facilities on Mudros were completely overwhelmed by the casualties, although the nurses valiantly struggled on. Fighting continued until August and by the 29th the campaign was over and had been an unmitigated failure. Many opportunities for attack had been missed in the general confusion. Neither side had really gained anything and 20,000 out of 70,000 men had lost their lives.

In December, my grandfather was at Sulva with Commander Unwin, evacuating everyone left. Unwin was aboard the last boat to leave the beach and when a soldier fell overboard, he dived in to rescue him. General Byng, the new IX Corps commander who was watching, said to Commodore Roger Keyes: 'You really must do something about Unwin. You should send him home; we want several little Unwins.'

Tucked into my grandmother's photograph album is a faded picture of my grandfather with Commander Unwin standing outside Buckingham Palace, proudly pinning on their new medals. In Unwin's case it was the Victoria Cross, and in my grandfather's the DSO. Behind them stands the upright, and rather forbidding, figure of my great grandmother, Mrs Morse, with a little lace cap on her head and her hands in a fur muff. The date written on the back was 15th January 1916.

Commander Unwin, Anthony and Mrs Morse

My grandfather wrote to his family:

H.M.S Napier
6th May 1916
Dear Family,

Am afraid I've been very bad with my letters but we have been very busy indeed & have had little opportunity. Dardanelles dinner was a huge success. We did not get it off until 28th but that did not matter. Our Table was really awfully nice and everybody admired the decorations. We managed to get some flowers at the eleventh hour. So all things went well. Our cook also excelled himself.

Re the question of leave & coming

to see the ship it will be when we go to refit probably June and I shall be able to tell you where we are. It will in all probability be where we were built – rather a long journey I fear. I shall be aboard for the first three of four days & then get away for about five or six. Not so bad at all.

For the rest we have had better weather but much fog & mist, which makes things difficult. I wonder if the "British Public" will ever realise what an enormous place the North Sea is and how limited an area even the colossal fleets of today can cover.

It is very sad about the "Kut"* force. How splendidly they have done. Of course from a military point of view the loss is not very serious but with the shortage of men one must deplore any loss particularly of such fine troops. What with Russell & Ireland we all ought to be depressed but up here people are more than usually "Cheery" and the odds are shorter than they have been for a long time. If only we could get a chance at the Huns what a difference it would make. I have nothing but admiration for the poor fellows up here who mostly have seen nothing at all and yet still are as keen as mustard. "Staleness" is an unknown quantity in the Fleet in spite of the "training" which they have been in for nearly two years now.

With love to all the Families

Yours

Antonio

Note:*Siege of Kut Al Amara (7 December 1915 – 29 April 1916), besieging of an 8,000 strong British-Indian garrison. Following the surrender of the garrison on 29 April 1916, the survivors of the siege were marched to imprisonment at Aleppo.

This was not long before he met my grandmother. Subsequently, there was an exhaustive enquiry in Parliament about why the British took on the Dardanelles campaign. Winston Churchill had to resign and did not return to the Admiralty until the Second World War. Sir Ian Hamilton retired. Colonel Mustapha Kemal, who successfully led the Turks at Anzac, later rose to fame and became the leader, Ataturk. The campaign is still used as an example of what not to do in terms of strategy, but nobody disputes the bravery of the men who fought there.

Chapter 8

The Meeting - 1916

'Nobody told me the name of the hero I was to encounter, but the date for the visit was fixed. I met Jack in London after arranging with 'Uncle' that my friend Phyllis would take my place on the Bum-boat. It was a long drive out to Campden Hill, and only as we neared our destination did Jack vouchsafe any information about our impending visit.

"I am not going to describe Anthony to you," he said, "because you'll soon see him for yourself and like him."

"I don't know about that," I answered a little nervously, "we shall see. What about the rest of the family?"

"Well, his Mother is charming, very quiet and gentle. She is a Quaker and a friend of Princess Louise."

"And his father?" I asked.

"He is a solicitor. Solid and reliable I should think. I hardly know him myself. I believe his children love him and find him a wonderful father."

"And the children, are there many?" I asked.

Mrs Sydney Morse

"Three sons, counting Anthony, who is much the youngest of the family, and one daughter. I should think she'll be there today."

We seemed to be driving uphill now so I asked if we were nearly there.

"Yes. They live in a great mansion of a house quite near to my old home in Campden Hill Square. Their house is filled from top to bottom with priceless pictures, old china and silver. It's like a museum."

This very much began to ring a bell and so I asked, "Do they, by any chance, live in Airlie Gardens, and is their name Morse?"

"Quite right," said Jack, "and here we are. Jump out."

And there we were standing in front of the same house that I had visited as a schoolgirl so long ago, when I had been so proud to be asked to tea by Enid, a friend older than me and so much higher up in the school. When the front door opened I felt like Rip Van Winkle. It was even the same parlour maid who stood there. The one who had so overawed me when I was a girl. She looked just the same and just as austere, except that she no longer wore the long streamers flying from her cap. But still the high, stiff collar supported her severe and uncompromising face. Even so, she seemed to unbend a little, and smiled quite benignly as she ushered us in. I realised this was probably due to the wonderful effect a naval uniform had on people in wartime.

The tea party went off without a hitch. Afterwards all I remembered about it was that I had never seen anyone with quite such clear, deep blue eyes. Anthony seemed typical of what a sailor should look and be. He was full of enthusiasm and vivid life and would obviously find nothing impossible to accomplish. He would push any difficulties to the winds and sail ahead and persuade you to do the same. He seemed reluctant to talk about his heroism but he did say how extraordinarily brave everyone who had fought had been, even the Turks, but that it had been a bloody battle. He especially praised the Australians and New

Zealanders. He then hinted that it was a clear example of bungling politicians sitting safely in their offices in Whitehall, ordering the 'troops' to fight in the places hundreds of miles away, in the Mediterranean or Africa; situations they were largely not able to comprehend, nor did they care as long as the war got won and the commodities were protected. I was a little taken aback to hear this opinion as I had never really thought about it. I tended to think politicians knew what they were doing, but when I came to know Anthony better I realized this was a favourite theme of his, one on which we did not always agree.

At about six o'clock, as Jack and I prepared to leave, Anthony asked me if I would join his party for a little dinner he was arranging that evening, for his Captain and his wife and a few friends. He gave us the name of the restaurant and said we would all go on to the theatre afterwards. It would be all quite easy and he would see to it that I got home safely. Would I come? I said I would love to. He seemed very pleased and explained that for the moment he must hurry away so as to be at the Admiralty soon after six, but said he would look forward to meeting again a little later on. I thought it an odd hour to be going to the Admiralty but later learnt that it was a very popular time for appointments, and many a Naval Officer would call at 'The Goat' or elsewhere on the way and get stuck there instead. Anthony obviously had not got stuck anywhere long because he had made every preparation for his evening party. When I arrived all was arranged to run on oiled wheels and I found myself whirled along without effort in an atmosphere of gaiety, which I was made to feel was entirely due to my presence. I felt very special and more than ready to enjoy everyone and everything that came along. In spite of it being wartime, we had a wonderful meal in a very smart restaurant in Belgravia. Soon after we found ourselves sitting in the stalls of a theatre enjoying the 'Bing Boys'. Everything was arranged with 'no fuss and bother', one of Anthony's favourite expressions that I came to know, when he was making any arrangements. 'The Bing Boys' had an eye for their audience and soon spotted our row in the stalls, naval uniform was more conspicuous in those days than khaki and had more prestige. What really drew their fire was the exceptionally responsive and loud laughter that came from our party appreciating every joke. Every now and then they would turn to us with a new sally, which seemed to have been made to fit the particular representatives of the Royal Navy now before them. They were so clever that, although they were probably making use of some of their well-worn chestnuts used on former young Naval officers, they seemed to us fresh and spontaneous, and we laughed and were merry and delighted. I thought Violet Loraine singing 'If you were the only boy in the world' was wonderful and was quite swept off my feet by the whole evening.

Before I got home that night somehow I found it was all fixed up that next morning I should help Anthony buy a dog. And so it was that together we entered one of the pet shops in Bond Street. The idea of acquiring a dog in Bond Street I found quite odd but intriguing, and had in fact, when passing the pet shop always wondered if anyone ever thought of buying an animal in such a manner. Now I found myself taking part in a doggy transaction and realized it was possible, obviously we were not the only one's who bought dogs in Bond Street! Perhaps it was not so unusual after all. We chose 'Shamus', an Irish terrier. He looked up at us so wistfully, as if he was asking to be bought and taken away from the stuffy little shop. I tried to persuade Anthony that the dog had no idea, poor fellow, that he was to exchange the shop existence for life aboard a ship; that even the most indulgent naval master could only promise his dog that he will be loved, well fed (too well fed), and petted by himself and all the sailors; but walks would be few and far between.

Anthony was firm: 'But I must have a dog to make me go walks when we get into harbour.'

I realized that he longed for the companionship and a friendly wagging tail to greet him in his cabin when he came down from keeping watch. Shamus proved a dear dog and Anthony loved him. The next day Anthony and the dog travelled back to Invergordon to join his ship. I was among those who went to see them off in their train. I noticed that Anthony's tie was pinned with a safety pin, and as he waved goodbye I thought 'I'll send him a gold tie pin; it will be a way of thanking him for the very pleasant time he's given me during his few days leave.' I bought the pin and posted it to him before I returned to the Isle of Wight.

When I got back and recounted my trip to London to "Uncle" he was a bit worried I was going follow in the footsteps of my two Thornycroft cousins and go and get married. He was not particularly impressed by my absence, or by the fact that we went to buy a dog.

'Seems to me, the fellow must have been hard put to it to take you to buy a dog in a London Shop. Couldn't he think of anything better to do?' was all he could gruffly say.

Not terribly long after the meeting in London I had a letter from Anthony saying they had been at sea for a while. When he arrived in harbour he had found my letter with the tie pin and that he was delighted with it. He invited me to accompany his sister, Enid, when she went up to Invergordon in October. He said that his ship was going to be in harbour for sometime and he would love to show me what a nice dog Shamus had become and Scotland was so lovely in October. The next day I had a letter from Enid saying she had just heard from Anthony, suggesting a visit to Invergordon for the two of us, and that he was sending her return tickets so we should not be bothered about buying them. He had also provisionally booked rooms for us at Novar House.

The journey to Scotland was not the simple and pleasant affair that it would normally have been in peacetime. We had not been able to book sleepers, but as we were starting very early in the morning that did not matter. We had our little red wartime passports in our pockets. Anthony's father, Sydney Morse, a picture of British solid reliability came to see us off at the station. He found us comfortable window seats opposite each other, arranged our suitcases with rugs on them, showing us how we could then stretch out if we felt like sleeping. Then he provided us with papers, magazines, fruit and chocolate and said goodbye. I did not remember my father, he had died when I was six, and I envied Enid. How wonderful to have a loving stalwart father to care for you! A man upon whose square, reliable shoulders his daughter could lean. And so, in truth, I came to know that Enid did, but also realized that in doing so, he over-filled the place that otherwise a husband might have taken in Enid's life. Although I hardly admitted it to myself, I had begun to think more seriously about marriage. I reflected that I was now 27, the war and the job I had with 'Uncle' and the Bumboats would not last forever, and I started to weigh it up. I found Anthony attractive and Jack was right – I had a great love of seafaring people.

We finally arrived at Inverness where there was a great fuss and to-do about passports and luggage and many questions as to where we were going and why. We satisfied the authorities that we were not German spies and were allowed to continue our journey. At last we were driving along the beautiful road that runs along the shores of Cromarty Firth. On the right, the Firth shone blue under the cloudless sunlit sky and we could hear the calls of many sea birds. On the left of the road the trees were turning, bright, vivid, autumn colours. Nowhere can September and October be more beautiful than in Scotland. The air is so clear and the sun so hot. The road seemed to go on and on for many miles without much variety and then, in the distance we saw a figure sitting on the bank under the trees. As we approached nearer we saw that it was a naval officer, who had now jumped up and was waving to us enthusiastically. It was Anthony, who had come to meet us at the entrance to where we were to stay. Novar House was a large family mansion that was being run as a hotel during the war, to house relations and friends of the Royal Navy. In those days the idea of turning your house into a hotel was unique, and the owners of Novar House were thought most revolutionary. It was surrounded by lovely grounds and was comfortable and warm with plenty of good food and staff.

I had bought myself a new dress from Debenham and Freebody. It was of stiff, thick, pale pink silk, with very thin criss-cross lines of black all over it and bunches of smudgy pink rosebuds at intervals. Remembering it now I feel a little embarrassed about it but at the time Anthony told me how much he liked it. The dining room at Novar House was a gay scene. It hardly seemed as if we were in the middle of a war. Round about a dozen small tables sat naval officers with their relations and friends. The tables were set with great care and polish and there were always beautiful fresh flowers.

The weather was particularly kind for October and we had picnics in glorious sunshine. I went for walks in the moonlight after dinner with Anthony and we talked late into the night, sitting in a hayloft over the stables. I would bicycle with Enid to Invergordon to visit Anthony's ship, and we were never prevented by rain. This bicycling made a great impression on my friends and relations at home when I wrote and told them. Something of great moment must be happening, they contended, to induce the usually lazy Marly to take so much exercise. After a particularly sunny, happy picnic on the hill, Anthony and I found ourselves sitting alone together surrounded by heather. It was our last day. Anthony asked me to marry him. When we rejoined the picnic party I was wearing his signet ring on my third finger.

Later back at the house I suddenly got cold feet and wondered what I had done. My dilemma was not made easier when I confided in Enid.

'I do hope," she said rather ominously, 'that you are not going to make Anthony unhappy.'

Marly before her marriage

Chapter 9

Marriage

'Back home in Westminster, listening to Big Ben from our little house in Lord North Street, Invergordon, the fleet and Anthony seemed a long way off, and the idea of marriage seemed a dream. When I felt the signet ring on my finger it would give me rather a shock, it was

a little daunting, but all my relations and friends seemed to think it was wonderful I was to be married.

Meanwhile Anthony managed to get a couple of days leave and came south, and we had a lovely gay time in London. Even so, I still had the troubled uncertain feeling as I walked away from his home on Campden Hill, after we had said goodbye and he left to go back to his ship. My mind was in a tumult. It was so pleasant being engaged, but did I want to be married? It was easy for Anthony. He did not need to alter his way of life at all. He would still be a sailor and go to sea with all his friends. But for me there would be a complete upheaval of my life. I should not even have a settled home, because, if I wanted to see anything of my husband, I would have to travel round and live in hotels or rented accommodation; and then with children? The fact that hundreds of other naval wives had done so was not much comfort.'

It seemed to me that now my grandmother had reached a trickier stage in her life. She lived at a time when the role of women in society was changing dramatically but marriage could easily put a stop to that adventure. For a woman marriage is a big decision to make, at any time, and she knew it. Edwardian society was bound by strict rules and before the war, only a few thought of the possibility of changing them. She had been healthily rebellious but was fairly conventional at heart. The First World War was changing the way women were regarded. My grandmother was aware of the suffragettes and the ideas they had; so far they had not been given the vote, as the War had interrupted the process. I thought about her and felt a lot of sympathy.

Even now in the post-feminist society in which we live, the dichotomy between being a wife and mother, and a person in your own right, can be confusing and finding a solution difficult amongst the many demands placed upon a woman. How did one make those choices? They were quite arbitrary really. Sometimes, you are quite sure or you have an absolute will to do a thing – you know it is part of your destiny. At other times, it is just taking the best option. Perhaps she sensed that she would find it hard to adjust, but for the time being she was caught up in the excitement of it all.

> *'When I arrived back in Lord North Street I found Mother in a very practical mood. She thought it was time that we put the announcement of the engagement in the 'Times'. This to me was the last straw, and she thought I was most unreasonable and perverse, as I would not agree to it. I tried to explain to her that I felt once an announcement was put in the 'Times', it would be quite irrevocable and that I needed more time to think. In the meantime, while I was thinking, I decided I would find work in one of the wartime Ministries. I got a job for a couple of weeks in the Ministry of Munitions but pretty soon realized I was drawing a salary for doing nothing useful at all, as I could not get the hang of filing the card indexes. My mother again broached the subject of the 'Times' announcement, and this time I told her I was writing to Anthony to say that I was so sorry but I did not think I would be a suitable wife for him. The immediate result of this was a telegram, followed by a letter enclosing a return ticket to Scotland, imploring me to come and discuss matters. This seemed only fair and*

reasonable, and so, as one of my Thornycroft cousins offered to come with me, off we went to Invergordon. We had a much easier journey than previously, this time we had a sleeper. Anthony and I had a lovely time and I came back completely reassured and fully engaged, with a carefully drawn up announcement all ready for my mother to send to the 'Times'. This was the 17th of March 1917.

At the end of March I suddenly heard from Anthony that he expected a few days leave over Easter and would that not be a good chance for us to be married? My future father-in-law, Sydney Morse, did not approve of marriages in Holy Week but somehow Mother was able to talk him out of his objections, in view of it being a wartime marriage. There were only about three weeks to make all the arrangements; even for a simple wedding, this took some doing. I decided on a white dress. Everything was quite a rush especially since we were at the same time giving up the house in Lord North Street. Isabel and John Thornycroft offered the hospitality of their house in Grosvenor Road overlooking the Thames, so we did everything from there. We were married in St George's Church in Hanover Square, on 5th April 1917. Anthony's Uncle Willie (The Rev Hon William Bowen) married us, and the two old friends who had introduced us were there – Jack Llewelyn Davies, as Anthony's best man and Commander Gerald Dickens, as a witness.

The Wedding (Commander Dickens on right with sword)

The Wedding (Jack Llewellyn Davies on left)

We had only four days for the honeymoon, which we spent in a charming "White Cottage" lent to us on the seashore in Bembridge. There was an added complication to be solved. A young maid, Maud Stevens, who had started to work aged fourteen with my aunt, and was now with Mother, decided she must come with me when she heard I was to be married.

"I go with Miss Marly," Nan (as she came to be known by my children) announced, "she'll never look after herself."

So we sent Nan on ahead of us to Bembridge to cook on the honeymoon. After this Anthony was to go to Saltburn where he was 'to build a ship', which meant he was to be in command of a ship while she was being completed, responsible for getting her and the crew seaworthy. Thanks to that we had the good fortune to prolong our honeymoon a little, living in a hotel nearby for a few weeks while the ship was being fitted out and loaded up with all the supplies necessary for fighting the War. Nan came too and I bought her some frilly muslin aprons and she became my 'lady's maid'. It did not take me long to realize like many Naval wives that I had a rival in my marriage, Anthony's ship and the Navy.'

Chapter 10

1918

"Thrones shatter, empires shake"
Goethe – East West Diwan

In 1918 the War ended when American troops were sent to help. President Woodrow Wilson, a pacifist, had refused to allow Americans to join in until April 1917. In March that year, Russia, with a Revolution to deal with, withdrew from the War and signed a truce with Germany. In July, the German offensive on the Western Front failed, and the British began to break through their defences in Turkey and Syria. In October, the German government appealed to President Wilson to start peace negotiations. In November 1917, the Balfour Declaration had granted Palestine as a homeland for the Jewish People, in exchange for support in winning the War. In the words of Lloyd George:

> "The Zionist leaders gave us a definite promise that, if the Allies committed themselves to giving facilities for the establishment of a national home for the Jews in Palestine, they would do their best to rally Jewish sentiment and support throughout the world to the Allied cause."

Two of President Wilson's main advisors were Zionist, and it was part of the plan to break up the Ottoman Empire.

On 11th November 1918, the Armistice was signed, and the Treaty of Versailles in August 1919. The League of Nations was set up. It was a utopian idea of Wilson's for which he was awarded the Nobel Peace Prize; with his 'Fourteen Points' he wanted to guarantee the independence of small nations, and *'end the folly and vanity of kings, and to any people ruling any people but themselves'*. It led Hillaire Belloc to write in 1920:

> "The old organisation of government by a commanding and an accepted class has gone forever. Nothing has yet taken its place...the desire of the bulk for Aristocratic government is clean gone, for good or ill, as a lost religion. With its passing and the passing at the same time of the Aristocratic class belonging to it, the whole nature of the State has suffered transformation."

The British and American Liberals attempted to impose "democracy" on Europe, by breaking up the Austro-Hungarian Empire and creating The Weimar Republic. Czechoslovakia was created as a nation state combining the Czechs and Slovaks; and Yugoslavia combined the Croats, Slovenes and Serbs (with no mention of the Bosnians, Montenegrins and Kosovans). Poland, regained its independence and Bulgaria was consolidated. It marked the end of the days of Kings, Tzars and Kaisers but in twenty odd years, it led to the Second World War. Winston Churchill was to write later in his diaries:

> '... unfortunately the men who made the 'Peace' did not hold together or have a concerted action and, as victors, they were unable to supply the necessary might, civilisation, learning and knowledge to ensure that peace. They lived from hand to mouth and day to day and from one

election to another until scarcely twenty years later the signal for the Second World War was given…'

In London, King George V and Queen Mary came out on the balcony of Buckingham Palace and waved to the celebrating multitude below. George V, unlike his flamboyant predecessor Edward VII, was a man of simple tastes, who disliked pomp and ritual. He had not expected to become King, until his older brother Albert died of pneumonia. He had spent his youth in the Navy and he was happiest at home in York Cottage on the Sandringham Estate, shooting and pursuing country pastimes. Nevertheless, he rose to the occasion; he had a tremendous sense of duty. He saw his role as king as that of a sort of feudal lord, and was the first British king who managed to form a link between himself and ordinary people, intelligently using the new medium of radio broadcasting. In private life, however, he was very rigid and stuck to strict pre-war conventional discipline, which probably led to the rebellion of his son and heir, Edward Prince of Wales, later the Duke of Windsor. King George V was obsessed with clothes and uniforms and looking 'the part'. Later in his reign, when the Labour Government was in power, Moss Bros was asked to ensure members of the government were suitably attired when they had interviews with him. 'Time keeping' was another of his preoccupations. In matters of government, however, he was remarkably flexible. After the Armistice the King went to the North of Scotland to review the Fleet and then, instead of spending Christmas quietly at Sandringham, he received President Wilson and his wife in London on their state visit.

My grandmother continues her story:

'Christmas that year was a real celebration. Jane had been born in June and was six months old, but we had a very gay time. The War was over and we set about

trying to get back to our normal lives, or what for Anthony and I was a new life. We all wanted to build a new and better world. Women over thirty were at last given the vote. The 'Stately Homes of England', as Noel Coward called them, opened their doors again and for a while life seemed one long party. Many 'Bright Young Things' started to throw all the rules aside and have a good time with a vengeance. There were people like the Mitford sister's, the Sitwell's and Evelyn Waugh: all clever, wild and unconventional. Edward, Prince of Wales, was a leader amongst them. He had incredible charm, was debonair and very popular. He seemed determined to throw over all the stuffy restrictions of his parents. Handsome and amusing, he appeared to follow in the footsteps of his grandfather Edward VII and get away with numerous affairs with older married women. It was thought perfectly acceptable for a man to 'sow his wild oats' or have a mistress if he was discreet about it. The same standards did not apply to women in those days, but there were young women who were trying to break free of the old world stigmas.

One sign of this was that fashions changed drastically. Stays and flounces became a thing of the past, thank goodness, and much more comfortable soft dresses, like Coco Chanel's first jumper suit, were the 'thing'. The more racy and unmarried girls flattened their bosoms to look like slim young boys, with short hair and short skirts, and were 'good chaps'. They wore make-up, smoked cigarettes, drank cocktails, slept around and did their best to be shocking. My version of the fashions was a little more staid and looking back at the photographs the tubular dresses seem rather hideous. But life was fun. We went to parties – house parties, shooting and tennis parties, Ascot and Cowes Week. The theatres opened again, and we played charades with friends for entertainment at home. Films and the wireless were still a great novelty.

*Beneath the gaiety, however, there seemed to be the aching wounds of the working class. The country was devastated by the effects of four years of war and terribly in debt. Although there were many people who still seemed very wealthy, or at least carried on as if they were, many began to have difficulties in maintaining their properties. The pre-war **1909** Liberal government's tax on land ownership came into effect. We knew people were obliged to sell off parts of their land, or borrow from banks something hardly anyone thought of before the War. No-one was able to employ the number of servants they had been used to, so many had been killed or wounded in the War, and those who were fit and able were not so keen to go back into 'service' after the equality of the War.'*

As 'The Man Who Won the War' Lloyd George was enthusiastically re-elected in 1918, promising to make Britain a 'country fit for heroes to live in'. At Versailles he had been mainly interested in repairing the damage to the British economy and had claimed compensation for the huge number of widows, orphans and men left unable to work, as a result of war injuries. The damage done by the War stretched much further than the battlefield. England was a changed nation. One in ten men under 45 had been killed; one in five wounded. The soldiers had been badly equipped, poorly trained and the conditions terrible. British fighting men all over the Empire had joined up with enthusiasm, and fought bravely and selflessly, in circumstances the horrors of which have never been equalled. Instead of an unequivocal devotion to those in command, many people felt that their commanders had sent men to their deaths unnecessarily. The aftermath of the War caused a quieter revolution in Britain than Russia, but nevertheless, there were big changes. The 'workforce' had gone out and faced death with all classes of men, and they were no longer prepared to put up with life as-it-had-been. Rising unemployment and strikes started to blight Lloyd George's time in office. He tried to grapple with many of the needs of the poor, initiating the Welfare State – *'the responsibility of the State towards it's citizens'* – increasing widows pensions, new housing, the National Health system and compulsory education to the age of 14. Women over 30 were granted the vote, after all the pre-war furore of the suffragettes. But Lloyd George found his hands full with Irish Home Rule and, very quickly it became clear that the Coalition could not cope with the post-war problems it faced.

'Anthony and I were not directly affected; we did not own any property, our lives were just beginning. We were comfortably off and relieved not to be at war anymore. We felt as if anything and everything was possible. Clyde was born in ***1920****, and named after the boat the SS River Clyde, although at first we called him Tony, like his father. Anthony was based in England on training ships, so it was not difficult for him to come home when he wanted. While the children were small we were able to enjoy a semblance of family life in rented*

accommodation. He continued to rise in the Navy, serving again on HMS Queen Elizabeth, while she was the flagship of the Atlantic Fleet.

In August 1922 he was promoted to Lieutenant Commander, and then in 1926, he was at Shotley in Suffolk on the Ganges, a boys' training ship. From time to time I managed to leave the children with Nan and join Anthony wherever his ship was. We had happy holidays, tennis parties, shooting and fishing in Scotland, skiing holidays in Adelboden and Chateaux d'Ouix; all the things that people did in the still 'gay' 1920's'.

Anthony with Jane and Clyde on board Queen Elizabeth

In June 1922 the Conservatives were able to prove the shocking fact that, in spite of his liberal views, Lloyd George had been selling knighthoods and peerages to raise money. Stanley Baldwin announced that he would no longer support a Coalition because Lloyd George was *'a dynamic force that was bringing destruction across politics'*. In the next General Election the Conservatives were returned with a majority. King George V, sensitive to the fate of his Russian cousin the Tzar (who had been executed in July 1918), chose Baldwin a self-made man, in lieu of Lord Curzon a peer of the realm, as Prime Minister. This marked a new trend in the leadership of the Conservative party, which had traditionally stayed in the hands of the aristocracy. Baldwin was a careful man whose motto was 'Safety First'. He became the ruling force for the next decade, apart from two brief unsuccessful attempts to lead the country by a new Labour Government under Ramsay MacDonald. Stanley Baldwin did much to improve education, public health, pensions, roads and public service, but in May 1926 a general strike indicated that it was not really enough; there was serious trouble brewing below the surface of the tremendously optimistic '20's'. For the time being, however, it was quickly solved. The *'Bright Young Things'*, mostly upper class students, rushed to volunteer to 'keep things going'. For them it was just another lark, driving a filthy train!

Chapter 11

The 1930' and the Rise of Hitler

Should I, after tea and cakes and ices,
Have the strength to force the moment to its crisis?
But though I have wept and fasted, wept and prayed,
Though I have seen my head (grown slightly bald) brought in upon a platter,
I am no prophet—and here's no great matter
I have seen the moment of my greatness flicker,
And I have seen the eternal Footman hold my coat, and snicker
And in short, I was afraid.
T.S. Eliot 'The Song of Alfred Prufrock'

'Anthony started to be sent away more frequently. In December 1927 he was made Commanding Officer of HMS Wanderer, a destroyer, and sent to China for six months. Sea jobs during peacetime were few and hard to come by, so most naval officers jumped at the chance of a job at sea and took them. I was good at occupying myself and had many friends and interests. After a while, however, the novelty of moving around wore off, and I started to find that staying in endless furnished rooms, or rented houses, was irksome and quite lonely, without Anthony to accompany me. It was difficult to manage two growing children in strange places; they needed to go to school apart from anything else. I had the faithful and efficient Nan with me, but it was not enough as the entourage grew more demanding. This way of life was

becoming too expensive and we decided in 1928 to buy a piece of land and settle down. Estates were being split up and parts sold off, so it was relatively cheap and easy to buy a piece of land and build a house on it. Like many Naval families we chose to live near Fareham, it was close to Portsmouth and the Solent.

Anthony and I had grand ideas for our new life and lacking any other example, I strove to emulate an ideal. I did not have much idea how to create at home with the children; my father died when I was very young, and I had grown up in exclusively female houses and we had been fairly nomadic. My mother had made a valiant attempt, she was energetic, resourceful, fairly unconventional and, most importantly, her own master. In retrospect, I think I rather made the mistake of imagining myself as an Edwardian lady, queen of the home, gracious, beautiful and good. Anthony never complained, but I knew he probably expected things to run 'with no fuss and bother'. Life in the Navy was quite grand for the officers. I was not used to running a large house and a hopeless cook. I had the help of the ever-faithful Nan, a gardener and chauffeur but between Anthony, the house, the servants and the children, I was beginning to lose sight of my own interests. I wanted to be a good wife and knew how much Anthony wanted a home, but I found when he was there, we had less and less in common.

It was not that Anthony was unkind or critical, but for him a 'home' was not something he was used to either. He had been in the Navy since he was eleven and he was relaxed in the company of his fellow officers. Home was somewhere he dreamed of in the cramped confines of his boat in hot faraway places, in grim battle – a green pastoral oasis of woods and hills, cuckoos and primroses. His world, I began to realize, was a fraternity of men who faced death together. It was on the high seas, in far off lands where Britain ruled the world, in the manly adventures of Rudyard Kipling and John Buchan.

I remembered one of the poems written by my cousin Siegfried, whose brother Hamo had been killed in Gallipoli.

Soldiers are citizens of death's grey land,
Drawing no dividend from time's to-morrows.
In the great hour of destiny they stand,
Each with his feuds, and jealousies, and sorrows.
Soldiers are sworn to action; they must win
Some flaming, fatal climax with their lives.
Soldiers are dreamers; when the guns begin
They think of firelit homes, clean beds and wives

I see them in foul dug-outs, gnawed by rats,
And in the ruined trenches, lashed with rain,
Dreaming of things they did with balls and bats,
And mocked by hopeless longing to regain
Bank-holidays, and picture shows, and spats,
And going to the office in the train.
Counter Attack 1918 Siegfried Sassoon

In Anthony's case, they had the excitement of a new port, its exotic attractions and the reverence with which they were treated, often like film stars. I knew he did not want to burden me with stories of slaughter and hardship, but I did rather wish he confided a little. He probably assumed I would not have been able to understand, but if he had tried to explain I might have known what he meant. From time to time I sometimes remembered Enid's stern injunction before we married, that she 'hoped I would not make Anthony unhappy'. It was perhaps awful to think it, but helping out with the war effort had been fun, and as a young unmarried woman I had had an unusual amount of freedom. I began to feel a little trapped.

In the 1930's our carefree life changed. The 'Crash' on Wall Street affected us all. People started to question their optimistic beliefs and wild behaviour. Friends with large estates were obliged to sell off parts to make ends meet. There was talk coming from America of the new Democratic President Roosevelt and his 'New Deal', that he blamed the economic crisis on the bankers and people borrowing too much money. But Germany seemed to be getting on its feet again. Adolph Hitler became Chancellor and there were magnificent marches in the streets. Many regarded him as the saviour of Germany, and some of our friends had met and admired him.'

It is sometimes difficult for us, with hindsight and the knowledge of what the Nazi regime did to the Jews, to understand why Hitler had such a following, even in England. Hitler had a brilliant, almost mesmeric gift as a speaker. As early as 1923, during the famous Beer Keller putsch, Dr. Karl Alexander von Mueller, a professor of modern history and political science at Munich University said:

"I cannot remember in my entire life such a change in the attitude of a crowd in a few minutes, almost a few seconds ... Hitler had

turned them inside out, as one turns a glove inside out, with a few sentences. It had almost something of hocus-pocus, or magic about it."

Many of the 'upper classes' were attracted by fascism before World War II. Since the Russian Revolution the idea of insurgence from below and the abolition of private property, terrorized many people in Western Europe. Aristocrats who were losing their land because of debt, found reassurance in fascism, when it seemed all the old values were being thrown away. In Italy, Mussolini saw fascism as a regime that was rooted in cultural tradition, recognizing the right of the individual, religion and family. His government supported the great estates, and an alliance between southern landowners and local fascisti thwarted peasant demands for land. He used his Blackshirts to repress socialist movements and strikes. He did not like Hitler and did not agree with Nazism, which had the element of racism, and only became an ally when he saw Hitler's success. In England, Sir Oswald Moseley became convinced by the ideas of fascism, and in 1931 launched a magazine called 'The New Party' with Sir Harold Nicholson, a respected upper class diplomat; the Prince of Wales and many of his smart set had much sympathy for Hitler and his ideas. In Austria, Vice Chancellor Prince Starhemberg, a conservative politician from the nobility flirted briefly with fascism; the Junkers, 'young lords' of East Germany and Prussia who had lost their estates, supported Hitler. A more ordered world had been wiped away by the First World War and its aftermath 'The Treaty of Versailles', and it was uncertain what would replace it.

'From July 1930 – Jan 1932 Anthony was made Executive Officer on HMS Repulse in the Atlantic Fleet based at Invergordon. Here he served under Rear Admiral Cunningham, affectionately known as ABC, with whom he was to serve during the Second World

War in the Mediterranean. Anthony told me he became aware of the financial sufferings of some of the navy personnel, when a mutiny almost broke out about pay cuts proposed by the Admiralty in an effort to deal with the Depression. In the end they were not carried out but it would have meant extreme hardship, especially among married sailors with families living on borderline poverty. Although Cunningham could be very strict about correct turnout and behaviour, Anthony witnessed his compassionate leadership, when he issued an open invitation for any rating with complaints to see him; he saw about 500 men individually adjusting their pay where he could.

The children were now old enough to go off to boarding schools. Jane went to North Foreland Lodge in Kent, and Clyde to West Downs in Winchester and then in 1934 to Dartmouth, to follow in his father's footsteps in the Navy. During the holidays we still went to dear old Bembridge and they rode and played tennis. We still all enjoyed fishing in Scotland, and Clyde shooting with Anthony, when he was on leave.'

Clyde and my grandmother with a salmon they caught

Jane on Bluebell

Tidworth 1933

In spite of my grandparent's happy times as the children were growing up, the 'thirties' was a dark and difficult time, not just financially. A mood of 'revolution' was sweeping the world. It caused everyone, from intellectuals to miners, to question what was left of the way of life that had been shattered by the last War. The horrors of battle had shaken many people's belief in God. Nietzsche had declared, "*God is Dead*". Although the Irish poet Louis MacNeice did not go that far, he said, *"God had gone round the corner"*. Just as some people found answers in nazism, others were attracted to communism and socialism. The philosophies of Marx and Engels, and the politics of Lenin and Trotsky started to fascinate radical thinkers in Europe and England. English writers like George Bernard Shaw and D.H Lawrence were concerned with social justice; Lawrence explored the concepts of changing attitudes to love, sex and marriage. The Bloomsbury group were questioning the extravagant values of Victorian England and its bourgeois social mores. Their ideas were feminist, socialist, pacifist and often atheist; they upheld individualism, creativity and personal enjoyment in their quest for meaning in life. Others were searching to make sense of the world in which they now found themselves in more mystical ways, people like Yeats, T.S. Eliot and Aldous Huxley. These ideas I know influenced my mother's thinking, when she was a little older and living in Oxford.

> *'During the term time, when the children were at school and Anthony was away at sea, I was very lonely. There were reports that Germany was re-arming and people were becoming concerned as to what was happening there. As the atmosphere became more ominous I felt increasingly fearful alone at home. Jane loved horses and was an extremely good rider with a 'natural seat'. She had made friends with a near*

neighbour, Nina Jelley, who bred ponies, which she rode for her in the local agricultural shows. Through Jane's passion for horses we became close friends with the family. Nina had a younger sister, Mary, an attractive and witty young woman of twenty-five. Although she was fifteen years younger than I, goodness I was now forty, I found her entertaining and very good company. She had a quick mind and a neat turn of phrase and was extremely practical, which I am not. She liked driving, gardening and was good at making things. She was not happy at home; her father was a very strict retired Brigadier, with four daughters whom he wished were sons. Of course, I had Nan who cooked, a daily maid, and a gardener who doubled as chauffer, but a large house in the country without enough staff to run it was quite a challenge. It was company I lacked more than anything else. I don't know who it was that suggested the idea that Mary come and live with me as a companion and chauffeur but it seemed a perfect solution and she rapidly became part of our family.'

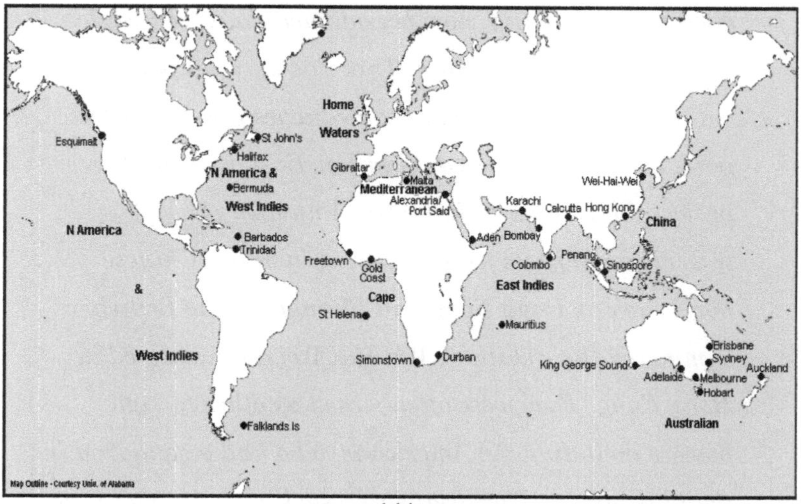

www.naval-history.net

Chapter 12

The Journey

"The superior man, when resting in safety, does not forget that danger may come.
When in a state of security he does not forget the possibility of ruin
When all is orderly, he does not forget that disorder may come.
Thus his person is not endangered, and his States and all their clans are preserved."
Confucius

'In 1935 we had the good fortune to escape from the gloomy uncertain atmosphere in England. We were invited to join Anthony in China, where he had been appointed head of the British Naval Mission. A trip to China was a wonderful adventure and it was all at the expense of General Chiang Kai-shek's government. Jane was 17 and had just left school.

Clyde was still at Dartmouth and unable to go so I asked if Mary Jelley, now my adopted daughter, could accompany us in his place. This was agreed upon.

European powers maintained warships in various ports in the Pacific Ocean and Far East, in order to protect their imperial interests. A number of international fleets were anchored in major Chinese ports such as Hong Kong and Shanghai. The British summered their ships at Wei Hai Wei and wintered in Hong Kong. They were often joined by other foreign powers including the Americans, who had a squadron in the Philippines. They were interested in trading with the Chinese, and keeping an eye on the Japanese. Anthony had already done a stint of six months in 1927 'showing the flag', and knew his way around a bit. The Chinese National Government had asked for British help in schooling the poorly trained and badly equipped Chinese Navy.

We came to know and admire General Chiang and his wife personally – at that time the British government considered him an intelligent and interesting military leader, although Anthony was a little wary of the amazingly complicated Chinese politics.'

My grandmother had little inkling of the unstable politics. China had been in a transitional state since 1911 and the fall of the Manchu monarchy. Chiang came from an upper-middle class family of salt merchants with a large estate, something of significance in an extremely class conscious China. He had fallen out with his mentor,

Sun Yat-sen, after he sent him on a trip to Russia, where he met Trotsky and developed an absolute hatred of communism.

Sun Yat-sen, was one of the founders of the KMT (Chinese Nationalist Party), and had a vision of a united socialist China. After a failed military coup to defeat the provisional President Yuan Shika in 1913, Sun was forced to flee to Japan. There he campaigned for Japanese support and was a revolutionary inspiration for many young Chinese. The small island of Japan was looking for raw materials and markets to sell its manufactured goods; the obvious choice was China. In August 1914, taking advantage of the outbreak of the First World War and their alliance with the Allies, with President Yuan's tacit agreement, twenty thousand Japanese soldiers crossed the Yellow Sea and landed in the northern Shantung area. By this time the Japanese had infiltrated local government in China, such as the police force. After Yuan Shika' s death, in 1917, Sun Yat-Sen returned to China and tried to unite the different factions, appealing to fellow communists the Russians for help. When Sun died in 1925, however, Chiang became the leader of the KMT and changed its policy. He was left with an inheritance of warlords created by Sun's opponent Yuan, many Japanese in positions of power, and a split party.

By 1928 he had consolidated his position but was still troubled by the warlords. He needed western backing to help him fight both them and the Japanese. Western governments, and more importantly, bankers were sympathetic. His wife, Madame Chiang, was considered an asset. She spoke perfect English, albeit with a slight Georgia accent (she had studied English literature in America), and said of herself: “The only thing Oriental about me is my face.” Many Americans reciprocated the esteem. Ernest Hemingway called her ‘the empress of China’, and the *New York Times* dubbed her ‘the most powerful woman in the world’. Eleanor Roosevelt was not quite so impressed and said:

"She can talk beautifully about democracy, but she does not know how to live it." Chiang did not share his wife's love affair with America; he was suspicious of their ambitions in China. The Americans considered him a tyrant who sent his wife to raise funds and irreverently called him 'General Cash-My-Check'. He preferred the English, hence probably my grandfather's presence.

General Chiang Kai-shek and his wife.

General Chiang Kai-shek and his wife

It was a trip of a lifetime and they faithfully recorded much of it on their brownie box cameras. The China they visited was before Chairman Mao and his communists had wiped out all traces of Chinese culture, In October of that year, Mao with his Red Army began the Long March north, challenging Chiang-Kai-shek and the warlords he was trying to unite. My grandmother was blithely unaware of the chaotic and muddled situation they were sailing into, but my grandfather must have thought it would be fairly safe, as he would never have allowed them to come.

My grandfather had written encouragingly on his journey out, only part of the letter remains:

P &O.S.N Co
S.S

...quite amazing conjurors.

We left at Noon & arrived Suez at 2.0 am the canal is awfully interesting both by day & by night (when its lit up by search lights on the bow of the ship and looks most lovely)

Left Suez 2 am & almost at once it began to get warmer by Thursday evening the swimming tank (canvas) was in commission & I had a glorious bathe about 6 p.m. Today Friday its Hot – not tropical – but the officers & men are in Whites & everyone is in summer clothes. It's a glorious day & I am very much looking forward to a second bathe at teatime. The sea continues as calm as a millpond, its very blue; & distant Arabia is mysterious & shimmering. I forgot to tell you that just after leaving Suez, the Arabian Shore is most weird & beautiful with gorgeous colours (reds, yellows & browns).

I had my first Chinese lesson this morning. Most interesting. The pronunciation is very alarming & will want a frightful lot of practice. Am only doing numerals at present. My Doctor thinks they are the best guide to pronunciation.

Saturday Hot today – it's a bit of a change when it first comes in. Its not really tropical but Hot everywhere – even the Breeze is hot & it doesn't cool you much. All the fans going. I slept comfortably last night with my fan half on & my shirt wound round my tummy. I haven't got a mat to sleep on. Don't *forget to bring one each – straw matting to go on top of your mattress. We get to Aden tomorrow & a large party including Enid & I are going a 10/-charabanc drive round Aden – to the Tanks & to the Oasis where there are lovely gardens. Time permitting we shall bathe in the swimming pool at Mohur (you get a very good little guide book given you all about each place before you get there...*

My Grandmother describes their journey:

'On October 11th having sold and packed up the Fareham house, Maylands, the three of us embarked on SS Ranchi in London. We were being treated to great luxury as it was one of the P&O 'R' class liners designed for pleasure trips to the Empire, with interiors done by Lord Inchcape's daughter, the actress and designer Elsie Mackay.

Jane at 17

We spent a couple of nights in London shopping and buying dresses for the tropics. Jane, ever practical, bought Horlicks dried milk tablets in case of shipwreck and a knife to protect herself from sharks! We caught the train from Liverpool Street amidst crowds of people who came to see off the boat train and arrived at Southampton Docks to board ship. As guests of the Chinese Government, our allotted cabins were generous, two 'de Luxe' cabins, one double with a private bathroom and lavatory for my 'daughters', and a single one next door for me. Jane was not particularly happy about having to share with Mary. I think she was rather jealous of her. Mary had spent a very gay time while they were in London, and to Jane's annoyance the cabin was inundated with bunches of flowers from admirers to bid her farewell.

Jane remarked somewhat wistfully, "Perhaps in a few years when I come out I will get 'bunched' too!"

On the first night of the journey down the Thames to Southampton the ship was full of creaks and shudderings and we all found it difficult to sleep. Mary suggested we cable Anthony and say we were not coming after all. Jane was horrified at this idea and persuaded us to overcome our doubts. The sight of many friends, who had come to Southampton to see us off, bringing more flowers and chocolates, cheered us along. The first day out at sea both Mary and I felt very seasick and Jane had to look after us.

The following day in the Bay of Biscay, she also succumbed to the much-famed Biscay 'roll' of the ship. There were only eight English sailors on board, the rest were all Lascars (East Indies) who looked very picturesque with their red caps and blue clothes, brown faces and gleaming white teeth but made me feel rather insecure – I did not fancy being shipwrecked with Lascars in charge.

Our first port of call was Gibraltar, where reassuringly two Royal Navy ships, HMS Hood and HMS Renown were lying in harbour. We were welcomed by the Governor and taken on a tour of the island for the day. A week later on October 18th, we arrived at Marseilles and were greeted by all the mail that had arrived with invitations for our arrival at Aden and Malta. We decided not to go ashore at Marseilles as the steward told us the town was 'a den of wickedness'. However, notwithstanding the dangers of Marseilles, the boat filled up with a more interesting crowd of passengers who, knowing the Bay of Biscay and its bad weather, had come overland to join the boat in the Mediterranean. This made the company aboard much more stimulating, and there were even a few flirtatious young men to amuse Jane and Mary. But now the heat started to become a problem. We had to spend most of the day on deck, as the cabin was very hot and stuffy. After luncheon we would rest on deck chairs but we found the lack of privacy and the noisy children running about very annoying. We played quoits on deck and tennis; in the evenings there were fancy dress parades and charades to keep everyone amused on the long journey.

The next stop was Malta, Malta that was to become in 1942 'the most bombed place on earth.' At this point, seven years earlier, all was peaceful. As we entered Grand Harbour we were able to recognize many friendly faces bobbing about in small boats, evidently waiting to come aboard. As our guests came up the gangway they all seemed to be carrying bunches of roses and parcels. From the ship we could just see the lovely old tenth century house where the Captain-in-charge and his wife lived. They were among our guests and asked us to stay with them for a week on our return journey. Everyone was so welcoming. Afterwards we realized it was not just ourselves who were so welcome but that we represented the latest link with home. All the ship's officers and servants came out in whites as we left Malta looking so smart, calm and British. It gave us a false sense of security before what turned out to be one of the worst storms we encountered during the whole voyage.

There were black skies, thunder and lightning and great heaving waves. We were all very sick. At 4.30 in the morning we arrived at Port Said and were relieved to disembark and go ashore to explore for a while. We were not impressed; Port Said was dirty and full of cheap tourist trinkets. Then on through the Suez Canal and the Red Sea, which was calm but extremely hot. In Aden we met an old naval friend who insisted, instead of us going ashore to visit, that he come aboard for lunch so that he could have an English meal and a break from Aden. Aden was an ancient natural harbour, still ruled as part of British India. The previous May they pulled out all the stops in celebration of the silver jubilee of King George V. For years it had been a way station for first the Portuguese, and then British on their trips East. Leaving Aden we sailed on to India in the Arabian Sea where we had two surprisingly cool and pleasant days, but then at Bombay many of the new friends we had made disembarked.

We were impressed by Bombay. At last we felt we were really beginning to see the world. We saw fine streets thronged with natives dressed in all sorts of gorgeous and beautiful colours, although intermingled with absolute filth and squalor in alleys and corners. At the Taj Hotel we ordered China tea (I always preferred it to Indian being lighter and more highly scented) and hot buttered toast, thinking finally we had found a place we could have the longed for tea. The toast was not a success, it was very thick and half burnt with no butter, and so we tried ordering cakes. A selection of brightly coloured Indian cakes arrived, one of which the more adventurous Jane tried and said tasted like a dust bomb. Off then to the 'Army and Navy Stores' and, in spite of most of the assistants being Indians, we were happy to find it was very similar to the one in Victoria Street in London. We found out that we could put things on my London account or pay with an English cheque, so we went to town and bought Elizabeth Arden face creams, biscuits and plum cake to supplement the poor teas on board ship. We found being treated like royalty by the 'resplendent' Indian porter was rather fun, and we finally sped back to the ship before sunset happy with our purchases. That evening we were invited to the Bombay Yacht club for dinner and had a delightful evening with handsome escorts. Back on board by 3.30 a.m. we were underway heading for the Equator where for some reason it became a little cooler and we all slept well.'

This xenophobic attitude to foreigners and travel seems rather preposterous, but for her generation, brought up at the end of the Edwardian era, it must have been quite normal. Certainly, my grandmother seemed rather carried away by her own importance on her first trip of any significance. Many English empire builders still regarded the world rather as their private huntin' and fishin' ground, with the inhabitants conveniently there as their servants. Either that, or foreign parts were mysterious, dangerous places and visiting was an adventure. It brought to mind Kipling, whom my grandfather loved so much. He put it aptly in his poem 'We and They':

All the people like us are We
And Everyone else is They.
And They live over the sea,
While We live over the way,
But – would you believe it?
– They look up to We
As only a sort of They!

My mother, Jane, told me many years later that she found this faint heartedness in the face of the unknown incredibly frustrating, but because she had no other company she had to make the best of it.

'On 4th November we arrived in Colombo (Sri Lanka) and bought lots of little wooden elephants from the natives who came out to meet the ship on small boats. The mail from home, which we so looked forward to, had also arrived. Among the letters we received an invitation from the Captain-in-charge, Sir Reginald Stubbs, for lunch. His little launch arrived rowed by natives who put up oars in a salute. We were taken

ashore and Sir Reginald greeted us in full regalia. A car was waiting to take us sightseeing wherever we liked. The wonderful trees and plants with humming-birds flying among the flowers made a great impression on me. We drove to Mount Lavinia to see the famous bathing Bay, the Club and the Galleface Hotel, where we managed finally to get a decent cup of tea, on a cool veranda in comfortable armchairs overlooking the sea. We all wished we could have stayed for a week in these benign and more familiar surroundings.

Back on board things were hot and stormy again. In the Bay of Bengal it was the monsoon season and we were caught in a storm. This passed and then there were beautiful nights under the stars with luminous flying fish. We were all touched by the romance of the journey. Penang delighted us with its smooth grass lawns and shady trees close to the sea. We had our first rickshaw ride, which I found quite terrifying as the rickshaw coolie decided to have a race with another rickshaw. Through the straits of Malacca, and then at Singapore, we had a short stop on Nov 9th when an old friend Major Hammond took us for breakfast at the Swimming Club. We finally had a chance to dress up and wear our pretty polka dot summer dresses and panama hats we had bought for the journey. He showed us around and later, on our return to the ship, joined us for a drink on board the Ranchi sitting on deck chairs. We found a letter from Anthony waiting for us saying he would come from Shanghai and meet us at Hong Kong.'

At swimming Club Singapore

On board Ranchi

Chapter 13

China

'The silk shared out in the Vermilion Hall
Was woven by hands of poor women
Women whose men were whipped in their own homes
By tax collectors who took the silk to court,
Behind those vermilion gates meat and wine go to waste
While out on the road lie the bones of men frozen to death.'
(Tu Fu 712-770)

'Approached from the sea, Hong Kong is an exciting city. It has all the exoticism of the East coupled with the security and convenience of an outpost of the British Empire. Important solid Victorian buildings, hotels and business premises cluster along the sea front with the Peak in the background. We stayed in the Gloucester Buildings where we were to return on our journey back. Anthony had been having such a good time while waiting for us that he had run out of money. I was a slightly annoyed at his extravagance and thoughtlessness, but it was not really a problem as we had brought plenty of cash with us, and he booked his cabin to accompany us on the next leg of the journey. That first evening we were invited to dinner at the Royal Naval Headquarters on HMS Tamar. We enjoyed the bustle of sightseeing in the city as we travelled around by taxi. There were hooting cars, rickshaws moving at high speed and two-wheeled carts being pulled by

Chinese coolies. British police, with benevolent composure, controlled this medley of traffic at the most controversial junctions. We did lots of shopping; buying beautifully embroidered silk lingerie, tablecloths and dressing-gowns, delicate blue and white rice-pattern china, a green porcelain tea set and lots of little Chinese figurines. I was pleased with the cheapness of everything, but my heart was distressed by the extreme poverty of the workers, and the contrast of the slums in which they lived to the other extravagant public side of the city. But I discovered this was not a new phenomenon.'

I had found many of these purchases when turning out my grandmother's attic at the cottage. They were still in the stiff 'Pukkah' suitcases from Harrods with cloth linings, their hardly torn labels stuck on for eternity with the pot fish glue used in those days, saying *"Peninsular & Oriental Steam Navigation Compy"* and *"P. &O.S.N. Co. Hong Kong"*. Some looked as if they had never been unwrapped. One in particular was a beautiful royal blue kimono made of thick raw silk, loosely woven in a basket weave pattern with large Chinese medallions within the weave; it was meticulously hand sewn with little cast brass buttons as the fastenings.

'Back on board ship we made our way through the Formosa (now Taiwan) Straits up the coast to Shanghai. During the night there was a violent storm. I clambered along the corridors to Anthony's cabin and climbed into his bunk and he took me into his arms. I was reassured by his calm and totally unperturbed presence. He was of course not at all worried.

Shanghai, at the mouth of the Yangtze, is China's major commercial port. It is the water route to Nanking and the interior. Small shallow draft vessels known as 'China gunboats' were constantly moving up river to concessions inland. We had been given princely accommodation at the enormous Cathay Hotel, which was the Chinese outpost of the wealthy businessman Sir Victor Sassoon's empire. Noel Coward was said to have written his play 'Private Lives' there and certainly it was glamorous; an Art Deco masterpiece fronting Shanghai's Bund waterfront. I did not really approve of Sir Victor, who was the undisputed king of real estate in Shanghai, as I had heard he had made his fortune out of the opium trade. I could not believe he was related to my second cousin Siegfried, however distantly. He was such a different character. He had none of the sensitivity and insight that I had come to know in Siegfried's war poetry and his delightful 'Memoirs of a Fox Hunting Man'. Sir Victor lived in sumptuous quarters under the hotel's green pyramid roof and was said to have four passions: beautiful women, thoroughbred horse-racing, Chinese art, and photography. He apparently once remarked: "There is only one race greater than the Jews, and that is the Derby." I found Shanghai elite rather hard to stomach. The British expatriates dominated it, with the Chinese social set slavishly aping their loudly voiced opinions. They sneered at Sir Victor because he was a Jew, but they seemed happy enough to accept his wealth and hospitality. Sir Victor threw costume parties in the ballroom at the top of the Cathay, and sumptuous meals were served in the hotel's very good restaurant. On our first night we were treated to an invitation to one of these balls. I declined as I was feeling very tired and said I felt ill; it was too soon to face a social evening. I found Sir Victor's habit of hosting dinner parties at 9 pm too late and preferred to eat alone much earlier. I was beginning to realize that foreign travel was not all it was trumped up to be, and missed the comforts of home. Jane had been quite tiresome and argued with me most of the time or sulked. Anthony was disappointed I did not join in the fun with the enthusiasm he hoped for, but soon went off happily with Jane and Mary. In all this luxury, to tell the truth, my fondest memory of the Cathay Hotel was of the Chinese 'Boy' of about 60, who on that evening and all those after it, faithfully sat on the floor outside my room in case I needed anything until the others came back from the night's entertainments. I find the older I get the simpler my tastes become. Sir Victor's Far East empire came to an end in 1941 when the Japanese took over the heart of Shanghai and occupied the Cathay Hotel. Sir Victor apparently took the change of fortunes philosophically, saying: "Well, there it is, I gave up India, and China gave me up!"

In spite of the comfort I did not really like Shanghai. It was a place of violent contrasts, everyone either so very rich or so very poor and much of the place filthy. The famous river Yangtze was disappointing. So wide was it that we could hardly see across to the other side. The waters were terrifyingly fast; they rushed by at such a speed and were a light mud colour, almost yellow. One day we lunched in our flag ship HMS Kent with Admiral Sir Frederick Dreyer, who told us that the sailors all wore life-jackets when employed on any work, in case they fell overboard. We were fascinated by the sampans, timber rafts and junks that lay closely packed together along the shores, inhabited by large families, their only roof protection seemed to be rush mats.

We decided to move on to Nanking. The journey by train, winding through paddy fields, I found quite awful. The carriages were much like our restaurant cars in England, except that they had spittoons placed at intervals down the side of the coaches that were frequently used. The Chinese, both men, women and children drank hot pale yellow tea out of tumblers into

which they dipped a little bag full of tea, jigging it up and down on a string, when they wanted the tea to become stronger. I wondered why no glasses cracked when the boiling water was poured in. As we travelled the Chinese attended to the requirements of their children, calmly holding them out over pots and wiping their bottoms on cloths that were eventually draped over the communal radiators! After a time we became accustomed to the stench. From time to time the train would suddenly come to a halt with a terrific clatter and steam from the engine, and armed soldiers with fixed bayonets boarded and began to search throughout the train. After much talking and pass-showing we were allowed to proceed. Apparently the railways were often held up but this time we were lucky.

Finally we reached Nanking and were taken from the station to the British Embassy by a smiling Chinese Naval Lieutenant in two horse drawn carts. It was November and already bitterly cold with the winds blowing down from Siberia. Our quarters were not ready but much to our relief we were served tea sitting by a fire. Nanking housed the Central Military Academy and was Chiang Kai-shek's centre of government. It was very different from Hong Kong or Shanghai. It felt like 'real China' and therefore much more difficult for European women. This made us nervous and unable to go out and about without an escort. We became aware of the noticeably precarious situation in China. The city was full of bandits or deserters, who had escaped from their unsatisfactory warlords and would raid foreigners as a way of living. In the Embassy, the staff's relations inhabited the kitchens and dining rooms at night, we would hear them below us shuffling and whispering as they took up their places to sleep. There was a regular village of people coming and going by the back entrance. Another problem was the water. We could not drink or even clean our teeth with it, unless it was boiled.

Chinese Officer Tsen

On our first evening there we were invited to dine at the Chinese Admiralty. We were very impressed by Chinese courtesy and ritual. Before dinner was served small brass finger bowls filled with hot water were brought, one for each person to wash his hands and a soft scented towel to dry them. There were two elegant and charming Chinese women in the party. They were expertly made up, something that impressed me as I had only recently started using make-up; my mother's generation considered it as being rather 'fast'. I usually just powdered my nose and used a little lipstick. The meal was nine-courses and at the beginning we struggled to eat with chopsticks until one of the boys brought forks. We had come forewarned, having already suffered at Chinese meals. We were armed with sponge bags specially bought for the purpose, which we kept on our laps and slipped anything we could not face eating such as unborn mice and fried locusts. At this particular meal there was nothing too revolting. On a previous occasion we had been served a whole roast suckling pig – most of the delicate morsels with which we were honoured somehow went into the sponge bag. Anthony was extremely worried that we were not up to the diplomatic task now before us and would embarrass him. However, we managed the sponge bags like adepts and there were no faux pas. Since he had warned us not to drink too much rice wine, we arranged to have our glasses that we were supposed to empty on each toast, filled with cold tea, and so managed to stay sober throughout these long occasions. After dinner we sat in a large comfortable reception room with an immense hand-made carpet, by a fire with huge logs.

The Chinese, even the distinguished and educated people, seemed to spit everywhere which we found disgusting. There were spittoons outside the entrances to most houses. In this congenial company we had a discussion about Chinese and English habits and this came up in the conversation. It led Jane, who had formed a rather naïve idea of Japan by listening to gramophone records of Gilbert and Sullivan's 'Mikado' to remark, "It seems to me that perhaps the Japanese would clean up China if they take over as they threaten."

This remark got quite a history lesson from an old Chinese academic who happened to overhear her.

"You have no idea what a threat the Japanese are to us. Firstly we have our own problems from the warlords; then there is Mao Tse-tung with his Red Army marching north. He has done a good job educating the vagabond element here and trying to curb the bandits, but if they become a large force they will be dangerous. The Japanese are far worse."

"In 1920 the Japanese were left out of the colonial carve-up, since when they have resented the Americans and Europeans. In 1923 Tokyo and the port of Yokohama were devastated in the Great Kanto Earthquake, and then Depression affected the Japanese economy in the same way as the rest of the world. More recently, to add insult to injury as you British say, the Americans restricted Japanese emigration to America, and the British have put tariffs on Japanese goods, saying they are produced in labour conditions not up to European and American standards."

Well I must say I agreed with that, having seen the conditions here, and I imagined it similar in Japan. I admired and liked the Chinese for their charming quiet manners, dignity and kindness with which they treated us. But I found the treatment of the half-starved coolies and the poor hard to understand.

The old man continued: "Now it is rumoured that the British want a naval base at Singapore which has upset the Japanese again. Since September 1931 they have occupied the Manchurian area of China, on pretext of quietening local disorders. The League of Nations told them to remove the troops, but they ignored this. We fought back, but we had no aeroplanes or weapons and had to withdraw. The Japanese have advanced as far as the Great Wall and the Americans have done nothing to help us. In March 1933 Japan withdrew from the League of Nations. So we are in a very precarious position."

Jane was a little taken aback that her attempt at light conversation had produced such a diatribe.

"They have no tradition of family life and moral virtue, and therefore we Chinese consider they are of no account and will never prevail over Chinese culture. No, no they are no good. They lack moral stability." He concluded, smiling enigmatically at Jane. Anthony was looking as if the he wished the floor would swallow him up.

We became good friends with many Chinese officials, including Admiral Wong, and a young naval officer Tsen, his wife and family of three girls who continued to send us photographs every Christmas.

Enid, ever adventurous and supportive of Anthony, came out and joined us for a while.

Enid on board with Chinese Officers

The Ning Hai Chinese Navy

Anthony was very busy a lot of the time with gunnery drilling on various Chinese ships.

Gunnery Training on board Ning Hia

We had pleasant times with other English ex-patriots and riding expeditions on the little Mongol horses that Jane loved. She bought countless porcelain and pottery statues of horses which all came back in the ship with us. Anthony, a keen photographer took pictures everywhere he went. We had an expedition to the Open Air Music Theatre in Nanking, although we did not go to a performance; in fact it was completely desolate of human life. We managed to get to the Ming Xiaoling Mausoleum, the burial ground of the Hongwu Emperor, founder of the Ming dynasty, which lies at the foot of 'The Purple Mountain' outside Nanking. Admiral Wong and Commanders Shee and Lee very kindly took us there.

Ming Tombs

Anthony was very impressed by the layout of the place and from that time developed an interest in Feng Shui, an idea not heard of in England at that time. He later used some of the ideas when working out the position of our new house at Chute Collis. The architecture of Chinese houses was of great interest to me too. I noticed that every house of any pretension had a number of courtyards, with the rooms opening out into an open-air area of privacy. The walls were tiled along the top, and at the entrance gate there was a porter's tiny lodge guarding the entry from all and sundry. There was great care to build all the important rooms facing south to catch the sun. On the outer perimeters there were gardens and blossom trees.

The political situation worsened and so we never managed our planned trip to Peking. We spent Christmas in Nanking and then we made our way back, returning to stay at the Gloucester Buildings in Hong Kong while waiting for our ship the Rajputana.'

Amongst my grandfather's letters was one to Clyde dated January 2nd 1936; it describes his view of the journey a little.

c/o Admiralty,
Nanking
Jan 2 1936

Dear Old Boy,

I am afraid I have not written to you for some time but hope this will greet you on your arrival at Dartmouth. We have been having awful weather here too and I am afraid it has not been very much fun for Mum and Jane. Mary has been ill with a cold or throat almost the whole time and both Mum, Jane have had colds too.

I had to go to Shanghai on business on Xmas Eve and intended to come back by the evening train. Owing to the "students" (communists) however no trains were running, things looked black for my Xmas dinner. I managed to get the last seat in an aeroplane leaving at 7.0 am on Xmas morning and was on the aerodrome at 6.30. Weather reports were so bad, however, that we were unable to start till 11.00. We were then turned back, owing to a snowstorm. At 12.30 the Down planes from Hankow & Peking came in and we started again and this time got through though very late and I did not get home till 4.30 having had no breakfast and no lunch!

We made up for it all right that evening. It was jolly lucky I got that seat as the trains were hung up for 3 days and no-one else got back till after Christmas! I may say the machine was American with an American pilot. I don't think I would have trusted myself to a Chinese that day.

All being well I am taking Mum and Family to Shanghai next Sunday and putting them onboard the *Carthage* (P&O) for Hongkong. They'll come on home in the *Rajputana* to Marseilles – thence by train to Calais due in London 23 or 24th Feb (address The Empress Club).

I have not been out shooting once since the Family arrived but am determined to chase duck or snipe after they have gone. Do hope you will have a good term and keep fit – it's the worst term in the year so be careful of yourself. I hope you had a good *leave and were able to get your gun fitted to suit you. I've done half my time here now so its not so terribly long before I shall be seeing you again. I'll be writing again soon but at present I am very busy getting the Family off.*

Very best wishes Old Boy.

Dads

He sounded somewhat relieved to see them all off.

On 11th January, the Sydney Morning Herald interviewed my grandfather, as advisor to the Chinese Navy for the past two years. He said:

> "China is training naval personnel in modern methods so that when money is available, key men will be ready to man the new ships. The manpower of the Chinese Navy is about 8,000. Most of them are Fukienese. They are very intelligent and quick on the uptake. They are excellent sailors and their drill is very smart. Of course the Chinese Navy's greatest need is money. More funds are necessary before expansion can be carried out."

The following December 1937 Nanking was the scene of one of the worst massacres in history, 'The Rape of Nanking'; an estimated 20,000 women were raped by the invading Japanese Army, and the city was burnt and pillaged. The Chinese army fled in chaos. The Japanese policy was 'Kill all. Burn all. Loot all.' His family had just got out in time.

Chapter 14

Coming Out

1936

'It was a relief to be back in London. It seemed so welcoming and comfortable after our travels. In our absence King George V had died, we had a new King – Edward VIII on the throne. We had a lot to do, as this year we were planning Jane should be presented at Court and have her 'Coming Out' dance. She seems to have benefited from the trip to China and surprisingly is not so defiant. She is enjoying the attention of photographers and dress fittings. I watched the transformation from an ugly duckling into a swan and can see she is much more confidant. We still do not see eye to eye on most things but I am glad that she is spreading her wings and enjoying life more. I sent her off to Paris for a short time to a Cordon Bleu cook so that she will not have the same problem as me. She came back with a book crammed with recipes, having had a thoroughly good time and she loves cooking. It will stand her in good stead.'

'The great day came on ***21st June 1936*** *and to our disappointment it was pouring with rain. Chaperones and debutantes nervously queued up outside*

Buckingham Palace dodging the puddles and sheltering under umbrellas, trying not to get their dresses and hats wet. It was really too much of the weather to be so inclement. Jane and Mary amongst them waited to be presented to the King. Although he is tremendously charismatic and charming, he seems to be intent on breaking with all the traditions his father and Queen Mary held to so firmly. He has already changed the evening Courts to afternoon garden parties. It is whispered that he considers the whole ceremony a farce, which is a pity, as it was an exciting moment for me and I love the pomp and ceremony of royalty; like Queen Mary, I feel we should hold on to our traditions. There is so much talk of republics and communists, and King George and Queen Mary have done such a good job of preserving our monarchy.

The King sat on the lawn under an awning with the other Royals behind him. Because of the awful weather it was hard to see him, but he seemed to scowl and hardly glanced at any of the young women who passed before him, each one curtseying as she had been taught. I was relieved Jane and Mary managed without any mishap. He is very handsome and I do admire him, and I dare say it is terribly boring for him to have to sit there especially in the cold weather.

"I wish at least he would pretend to be pleased to see us, but I suppose he is not used to it," whispered Mary to Jane.

Jane, less impressed by royalty, replied somewhat disrespectfully, "I expect he is wishing he is with Mrs Simpson and not having to look at all of us."

In March of 1937 my mother died. The children dearly loved 'Gags', as they called her. We have decided to postpone the dance until the summer. Anthony will be able to be there, and we can have it on board his ship HMS Curlew, at Chatham. The King has abdicated to marry the love of his life Wallis Simpson, so probably his bad mood had nothing to do with the young women who were curtseying to him. The abdication has all been very distressing and I do not care for what I have heard of Mrs Simpson, who seemed intent on destroying the King's life. Why could she not just go away quietly and with dignity? It was a painful and puzzling time for everyone who watched the drama as it played out. What a blessing it is that the former Duke of York has become King George VI, with his wonderful Queen Elizabeth at his side. They are doing a tremendous job and reassuring the country that everything will be all right. Anthony knows him quite well and likes him very much; they had coincided at Osborne, Dartmouth and later in the Navy.

The dance was a great success. A debutante's ball on board ship was quite a novelty. The Navy took over and I was relieved of most of the arrangements. Like Lord Nelson, I am a firm believer that "nothing is too much for the Royal Navy!" Everything was organized to perfection. Little fairy lights lit up each side of the road through the dockyard; at the slightest hitch there was a helpful sailor on hand. We danced to Jack Jackson's band. Jane looked lovely, and I have copies of her in the romantically blurred photographs that appeared in the 'Evening Standard', youthful and full of hope, her hair crimped in the fashionable shingle close to her head.

Jane as a Debutante

Her face is a perfect oval with her father's high cheekbones and a little button nose that came from neither of us, although my sister Dinny has a more snub nose than me. For the ball she wore a cream satin dress. She is still a little shy, but has lost her puppy fat since the trip to China, and her satin dress showed off her good figure to advantage. She is enjoying plenty of invitations and social life.

Jane at Deb Dance

The Naval officers were in full regalia with their medals and bow ties. Clyde, now a Midshipman, thoroughly enjoyed himself. He was much in demand with his good looks and height, and he is less worried about what people think of him than Jane. He has his father's high forehead, straight nose and sensitive face, the same cheekbones and the arresting eyes, with which I had fallen in love and still sometimes seem to pierce through to my heart. Clyde threw himself into every opportunity for fun and gaiety; he is very endearing and witty and has a way of saying things that makes everyone laugh. At the same time he is always extremely thoughtful of other people's needs.

Clyde as a Midshipman

We still have to finalize our plans for the house in Chute. The flat in Halkin Place is very convenient and a good base, although it is small if we are all there at the same time. It is spacious and light with lovely parquet floors, and there is a small roof garden, where we can sit out on chairs and have some plants in boxes. The porter on the ground floor is always so kind and helpful with shopping and parcels; his splendid uniform almost outshines the doorman at Harrods, just around the corner. It is a useful pied-a-terre and convenient for Anthony when he needs to be at the Admiralty. But we need a house in the country again and most of our things are in storage. London has developed fast since the Armistice in 1918 and is very busy and overcrowded. In winter everyone burns coal so there are terrible pea-soup fogs. I worry about tuberculosis; doctors are trying to eradicate it by providing antibiotics, but I do not really trust them, I believe in prevention rather than the cure. The milkman with his horse and float, clip-clopping along the streets rattling with the bottles of milk, is one of the welcome sounds of early morning London, but the dairy is not obliged to pasteurize its milk, so I insist Nan boils it to be on the safe side.

We have found land on the healthy and exhilarating chalk downs of Wiltshire, not far from Stonehenge. It exemplifies everything that Anthony and I think of as England. It is a soft expansive landscape with undulating hills and whaleback ridges. The beech trees, in isolated circles, break the horizon. In early spring during lambing, the bleating sheep surround the lonely shepherd's huts; their music orchestrated by the forlorn cry of the lark as it rises high in the sky. Little villages nestle in the dales amongst the downs. It all seems far from the strife and threats of modern life. Anthony, using some of the Feng Shui ideas he learnt in China, has picked out a perfect spot for the house, just outside the tiny village of Upper Chute. He is to be stationed in South Africa for the next three years and is laying out plans for the house before he leaves. We plan to fill it with Jane and Clyde's young friends. Jane is now away at the Slade School of Art, and Clyde still at Dartmouth, but they both want somewhere to invite their friends. Since the idea is that the house should accommodate lots of guests, Anthony says that means lots of baths. It is to have seven bedrooms and four bathrooms, which seem to me a little excessive, but he is probably right and I do not want to quibble. The design is red brick, what they now call mock Georgian. There will be room for a paddock for the three ponies, a croquet lawn and tennis court, and good shooting for Anthony and Clyde – deer, pheasant and partridge and, failing them, plenty of rabbits. An old roman road, lined by yew trees along the ancient pilgrim route between Salisbury and Winchester, dips up and down the hills in a straight line past Stonehenge; motoring back and forth to London and Portsmouth should be easy. Mary, Nan and I all plan to camp out in individual little garden huts, to keep an eye on things while the building is being done, with brief sorties back to London for a bit of luxury.'

A little later she writes:

'In London the threat of war is becoming more ominous and there is a lot of talk of Hitler's rise to power. When we listen to the wireless the news is not good. The Germans have withdrawn from the League of

Nations and there are rumours that Hitler is training a large Air Force. Our government does not seem to be in control and there is a constant talk of imminent war, even though most people do not want to believe it. People coming back from Europe are saying that the Jews are being persecuted and made to leave their homes and businesses. Nobody wants another war; it seems impossible to believe it is happening so soon, when we have just recovered from the last one. Jane told me she saw newsreels the Spanish town of Guernica being bombed by the Luftwaffe, Hitler's new Air Force. It brings home that we could be threatened in our homes at any given moment, and the Navy could not defend us, as in the past. The idea of being attacked from the air is worrying. I remember at the end of the last war, the Germans dropped bombs around Liverpool Street Station, causing many casualties. Mr Baldwin is pessimistic and says, 'the bomber will always get through'.

In this uncertain atmosphere, Stanley Baldwin, after handling the abdication of King Edward VIII and the crowning of King George VI in May 1937 retired, worn out by life in office. Neville Chamberlain became leader of the Conservative Party, and was in the words of increasingly exasperated Churchill:

"...Alert, businesslike, opinionated and self-confident in a very high degree. Unlike Baldwin, he conceived himself able to comprehend the whole field of Europe, and indeed the world. Instead of a vague but none the less deep-seated intuition, we had now a narrow, hard-edged efficiency within the limits of the policy in which he believed...his all-pervading hope was to go down in history as the great Peacemaker...he was imbued with a sense of a special and personal mission to come to friendly terms with the Dictators of Italy and Germany."

'In July Anthony went off to the Union of South Africa. I know I am no different from other wives of Naval personnel who are doing their duty but I wish he were not so far away. I am, however, thankful he is out of danger's way. It is a worrying situation and is becoming grimmer every day.

There is a government campaign to encourage people to make themselves air raid shelters and dig trenches in their gardens. Sir John Anderson's Civil Defence has issued Air Raid Precautions (ARP) as to how to prepare your house for the blackout and how to behave in case of attack. There are constant reminders and advice in magazines, and people are volunteering for posts as local wardens in case of panic. There is also talk of poison gas and so even cigarette cards, which Mary collects, have instructions for avoiding contamination by mustard gas. Gas masks are being issued and we are advised to keep them beside the bed at all times. Although life goes on as usual, it is worrying and we need to get to Chute.'

In February 1938 Anthony Eden, backed by Churchill, resigned as Foreign Minister. Churchill had repeated disagreements in Parliament with Neville Chamberlain and his fellow 'appeasers' in the House of Commons, about Britain's preparedness for war. Churchill wanted to make it clear that the Allied governments, and most of their populations, had lulled themselves into a false sense of security.

This was because in 1932, at a League of Nations disarmament conference, it had been decided on a policy of 'qualitative disarmament': banning 'aggressive armaments' but allowing 'defensive ones'. President Roosevelt, who did not attend, had sent a message to the Conference saying:

"If all nations will agree to eliminate from use the weapons which make possible a successful attack, defences automatically will become impregnable and the frontiers and independence of every nation will become secure."

But he made it clear that America, in the grips of the Depression and race riots in the South, did not wish to become involved with Europe's quarrels. The agreement had meant that the British Navy was down to 50 cruisers, 120 destroyers and only 3 battleships to police a world Empire. They were not ready to fight a war and defend Britain. Since Hitler had come to power his belligerence was worrying. France had wanted assurance that her old enemy, Germany, was disarming with the rest of them, but Hitler had refused to accept the French conditions. In October 1933 he had withdrawn from the League of Nations. The American Consul in Berlin reported that Germany:

"...although making constant professions of a will for peace and a desire to cooperate, would 'fight shy of all conferences' on disarmament".

In the meantime Germany had been rearming. She had rapidly developed her Luftwaffe, and in 1934 when the British Foreign secretary visited Germany, he reported that the German Air Force was well equal to that of Britain's. In 1936 the number of Germans undergoing regular military training was 1,511,000 men and women, compared to 623,00 Frenchmen, only 407,000 of whom were in France, the remainder were in French colonies. When in 1936, Hitler moved to re-occupy the demilitarised zone of the Rhineland, his more moderate generals, alarmed at his disregard for the Versailles Treaty, had tried to keep a check on his meteoric rise to power. They did not want to provoke another European war, which seemed impossible to win.

In 1937, although Churchill was accused of being alarmist by many of Neville Chamberlain's government, it became obvious that they were heading for a war. Sir Philip Cunliffe-Lister, now head of the Air Ministry, found unused prototype designs of Hurricane and Spitfire fighters left by his predecessor Lord Londonderry, and immediately started to mass-produce them. He invited Churchill to be part of the Committee on Air Defence Research, finally ending what Churchill called his 'Wilderness Years' – since his disgrace over the Dardanelles in 1915. Churchill enthusiastically went into action and called on the help and advice of Professor Lindemann, a brilliant German-Jewish atomic scientist from Oxford, who hated Nazi Germany. By the time war broke out, Britain still had about half the number of planes of Germany, but they were of high quality and were, by then, in fast production. England was also making breakthroughs developing ideas of Radio Direction Finding (later called RADAR) for the use of aircraft detection and shipping, which proved to be of immense value to the Allies' success in the coming war.

Hitler had not really planned on a general war involving Britain and certainly had not prepared his Navy, The agreement had been that the German Navy should not exceed one-third of the British Navy, however, this did not include U-boats or submarines. The British Fleet was better prepared but had many fronts on which it had to operate, and Britain's defence had always depended on her Navy. It was vital for her to 'rule the seas' – her wealth and very existence came from imports and exports. As Sir Basil Liddell Hart, military correspondent for the 'Times' said:

> "There are some twenty basic products essential for war: coal for general production; petroleum for motive power; cotton for explosives; wool; iron; rubber for

> transport; copper for general armament and all electrical equipment; nickel for steel-making and ammunition; lead for ammunition; glycerine for dynamite; cellulose for smokeless powers; mercury for detonators; aluminium for aircraft; platinum for chemical apparatus; antimony, manganese etc., for steel-making and metallurgy in general; asbestos for munitions and machinery; mica as an insulator; nitric acid and sulphur for explosives. Except for coal, Britain lacked most of these products in quantity. As long as the use of the sea was ensured by the Navy, most of them were available in the British Empire.... apart from which, the best placed of all the powers was the United States."

On 12th March 1938, Hitler marched triumphantly and peacefully into Vienna, where 200,000 people cheered and showered him with flowers in welcome, in what was known as "Blumen Kreig". The Nazi Party had infiltrated members into positions of power in Austria, and people were expecting a ray of hope in the economic crisis. Neville Chamberlain, for Britain protested but did little more, giving tacit license to the bold move.

Chapter 15

South Africa

"The continuance of the Versailles status is becoming an offence to the conscience of Europe and a danger to future peace..."
General Smuts

My grandfather was now Captain J.A.V. Morse D.S.O. of the light cruiser *H.M.S.Neptune,* and Commanding Officer, Africa Station 6th Cruiser Squadron. He was part of South Atlantic Command based at Freetown, Sierra Leone, serving under Vice Admiral George H D'Oyly Lyon. The job was to patrol the South Atlantic and keep the vital trade routes open.

He was stationed at Simonstown. It could have been an English seaside town with a Naval Base. Many parts of the Cape must have reminded him of the Isle of Wight, the little Victorian houses with verandas, or stoeps as they call them there. The Navy spent much of their spare time in Cape Town where they could enjoy a more elegant life. There were dinners, sophisticated company and comfortable hotels like the Mount Nelson, where they could almost feel they were back in London. Before the opening of the Suez Canal, Cape Town had been the traditional port of call for ships that had to take the long route East. I spent 12 happy years living there and appreciated what my grandfather must have felt for the place. The beautiful natural harbour at the foot of Table Mountain, with its flat top and 'tablecloth' of clouds falling over its steep sides, had always been an ideal spot for men on active service, existing from day to day in storms and big waves, to anchor, for a short run on dry land while refuelling. Supplies of fresh fruit and vegetables were plentiful and, in days gone by, they could adjust their compasses. For my grandfather, the terrain must have seemed more majestic and harsh than their new home in Wiltshire; instead of clumps of beech trees clustered on hilltops, here the wind bent the trees almost over backwards, resisting the years of Cape winds only by their flexibility. In many ways it was reminiscent of his beloved Scotland; the fynbos was just heather on a gigantic scale, and it had the same rugged dignity, but of course much shorter winters. Apart from the stunning natural beauty of the place, there were most of the familiar comforts of home. The South Africans were warm and friendly hosts who did not have the stiff protocol of the English. From the tone of the letters he wrote and those he kept, he liked South Africa and obviously made many good friends, especially at Admiralty House in Simonstown, where he was training the South African Navy. The building tensions of Europe must have felt quite far away.

Among those he came to know was the Prime Minister of South Africa, the brilliant philosopher, statesman and botanist, General Smuts, who had served with Winston Churchill in the previous war. Smuts, like Neville Chamberlain and many people at that time, was in favour of appeasement. In 1934 he said to an audience at the Royal Institute of International Affairs:

> "How can the inferiority complex which is … I fear, poisoning the mind of Germany be removed? There is only one way, and that is to recognize her complete equality of status with her fellows …While one understands and sympathizes with French fears, one cannot, but feel for Germany in the prison of inferiority in which she still remains, sixteen years after the conclusion of the war. The continuance of the Versailles status is becoming an offence to the conscience of Europe and a danger to future peace...Fair play, sportsmanship-indeed every standard of private and public life, calls for frank revision of the situation. Indeed, ordinary prudence makes it imperative. Let

us break these bonds and set the complexed, obsessed soul free in a decent human way, and Europe will reap a rich reward in tranquility, security and returning prosperity."

Once living in South Africa, he must have realized that Smuts, in spite of his popularity in England, was not so admired by non-white South Africans or, the Africaaners who were often pro-German. He probably mostly socialized with the English South Africans. At that time, Smuts was advocating a segregated society, fearing that giving black Africans the vote would herald the destruction of Western civilization in South Africa saying:

> "These children of nature have not the inner toughness and persistence of the European, not those social and moral incentives to progress, which have built up European civilization in a comparatively short period."

Smuts lost the 1948 election in South Africa when apartheid was established, but many of the laws he had previously put in place to protect white supremacy continued. He died two years later and so never witnessed the consequences of his ideas.

HMS Amphion with Table Mountain in background

In August 1938, when my grandfather had been in South Africa for a year, Clyde finished at Dartmouth and went out to join him on the *HMS Amphion*, a training ship. My grandfather was obviously delighted and proud to have his now adult son serving under him. They had spent so little of Clyde's life together. There were regular sorties patrolling the Atlantic. On various journeys, while the ship was wending its slow way up and down the West Coast of Africa, Clyde, who was a good letter writer, corresponded regularly with his mother. He wrote:

H.M.S. Amphion,
AFRICA STATION.

At sea *August 7th*

Dear Mother,

Our trip to LUANDA (Angola) was more political than entertaining. Although I had one evening's duck flighting, which in spite of the mosquitoes was good fun, I would rather have stayed at Simonstown with regular mails.

When the President of the Portuguese Republic arrived, there were terrific celebrations in the town and roars of "Viva! Viva! Viva Carmona!" intermittent firing of guns, rockets and fireworks, small aeroplanes dropping thousands of leaflets (most of which went into the sea) and small pieces of greenery. Real excitement ran high amongst the white population. The natives caught crowd hysteria and cheered like anything but I doubt if they knew why.

Our part of it was confined to firing 21 gun salutes at every possible moment and sending boats to escort his barge to, and from, the liner ANGOLA which he came and left in. On our last day he came onboard and we had an inspection. He is a funny, wizened little man of about seventy with a bristly little white moustache — very short. Afterwards we had a sort of "at home" to which a great many of the locals came. French was the language I found most useful (running over my stock!!) and I fairly jabbered away. Very few of them spoke English (ignorant chawbacons!) and some 'had' no French either.

Today we meet Dad in his battle-boat after doing a hide-and-seek exercise with him this morning. After some more goings-on we get back to snookey some time tomorrow afternoon. There we should find no less than five airmails waiting for us with a good many for me I hope.

The wind seems to blow in the direction of my coming home in a liner after our exams in early October which would be excellent but one hears so many stories that one does not know which to believe.

However I wouldn't be looking the gift h in the m – but I'm afraid the Admiralty won't spend fifty pounds on giving me a months' extra leave – we shall see.

It being August I should think there must be some mushrooms in evidence – I hope you are enjoying them. This 'ere boat is beginning to put on speed (must have seen the Neptune) and the vibration is making writing even worse so I will stop.

lots of love from Clyde.

Anthony in South Africa

1st Sept 1938

H.M.S. Amphion,
AFRICA STATION.
P.E. (Port Elizabeth)

Dear Mummy,

Thank you very much for your last epistle, coming as it did from Bonny Bournemouth on the sunny South Coast!

We have just arrived at this 'ere Port Elizabeth which is not at all a bad spot – good shops quite close and a terrific snake Park which I am going to inspect this evening. We only spent a very few days at Simonstown before coming here but Dad and I managed to go to the Races together. It was good fun – all the Wealth and Beauty (much!) and a very nice stand with a green lawn – Their Excellencies being present plus entourage etc. I did not wear a hat, as I dislike them, so I got a good old raspberry from Bob on the next day. He had been at the meeting with the CinC and had lost his dough! – laugh!

I just backed my fancy and did very well, just couldn't back the wrong one! The headmistress of a riding school on a black horse did very well for me. It was the ladies and the last race. I plunked my all on her and she brought home the bacon and £-10-0 for me. I was £2-10-0 up in the end – very lucky.

I have met some people here called Merryweather, the man was in Dad's term at Dartmouth. They have asked me to go out to their farm at ADDO (35 miles from here approx) and stay from Saturday afternoon to Sunday evening. It should be very pleasant as they are most "homely" people. I think Dad spent a day or two out there. When we get back to Simonstown this time, it will be for the last time – a good thought.

I'll be seein' you! lots of love from Clyde

Meanwhile back in Europe Hitler was demanding the return of the Sudetenland, the German part of Czechoslovakia. He regarded the Czech state as a multi-ethnic mongrel state (it was made up of Czechs, Germans, Hungarians, Slovaks and Poles) giving the lie to Versailles Treaty's intention 'of the right of small nations to govern themselves'. It was also the home of most of the banks, and, all the defences in the form of mountain forts; if he succeeded he would gain control over the rest of Czechoslovakia. At the time a group of Hitler's alarmed General Staff were plotting a military coup to arrest him, feeling quite sure that he would provoke another war. This was, however, thwarted because on 29th Sept 1938, Neville Chamberlain asked Mussolini to persuade Hitler to come to a meeting with Edouard Daladier for France, at Munich. There it was agreed that Hitler would be granted his wish for Sudetenland, in exchange for a promise that he would advance no further. Nobody thought it necessary to invite the Czech government, who were informed of a *fait accompli* at 1.30 on the morning of 1st October. At the last minute, Hitler almost did not sign the treaty, saying that there was no ink in the inkstand; this was rectified to everyone's relief. The next morning Neville Chamberlain had a private meeting with Hitler, signing a piece of paper agreeing that Germany and Britain would 'never go to war with one another again.'

For Chamberlain, the Munich Agreement spelt 'peace for our time'. He returned to inform the King and wave to rejoicing multitudes from the balcony of Buckingham Palace. He seemed to have prevented a war. He addressed the nation by radio, and after thanking those who wrote congratulating him, said:

> "How horrible, fantastic, incredible it is that we should be digging trenches and trying on gas-masks here because of a quarrel in a far-away country between people of whom we know nothing. It seems still more impossible that a quarrel that has already been settled in principle should be the subject of war."

Winston Churchill and Anthony Eden, however, were furious, saying Britain had behaved dishonourably to the Czechs. It gave Hitler the confidence to carry on with his plan for *lebensraum* – 'more agriculturally useful space' for Germany and triumph over his rebellious generals. When, later that day, the German Foreign Minister Joachim von Ribbentrop remonstrated with Hitler for signing the piece of paper with Chamberlain on his own, the Führer replied:

> "Oh, don't take it so seriously. That piece of paper is of no further significance whatever. If ever that silly old man (Chamberlain) comes interfering here again with his umbrella, I'll kick him downstairs and jump on his stomach in front of the photographers".

In one of his public speeches after Munich, Hitler declared:

> "Thank God we have no umbrella politicians in this country".

After the news of Neville Chamberlain's meeting with Hitler and the Munich Agreement, there was a momentary general relief throughout Britain and the Armed Forces, and Clyde wrote to his mother:

Oct 12th 1938

HMS Amphion
Africa Station

Dear Mummy,

Well ....thank heavens all this war is over and you must be relieved at home. Dad & I were certain ou'd hop down Chute way, so did not worry about bombs etc!

I just long to see you and your country mansion – we leave here in ten days' time, a good thought! – it's funny but I feel sorry to leave, what with Dad being here and the summer coming on, and yet I long to be home, so where am I ?

We are in the midst of our exams. Two are past, but the biggest comes in three day's time.

..............TIME PASSES..............

I was in such a p'other about exams that I did not finish off this letter to you. We have all passed (sigh of relief!) I got 82%, which gives me a 2nd class – if only I had got 85% I would have got a First! It's a pity but I won't let it get me down! I'm not certain, but I think you may now address me as "Acting Sub-Lieutenant Morse" – but Midshipman, for short, is easier to write! Last night I spent in Dad's sea cabin and in about twenty minutes we set off for Hermanus. It should be a good drive, as the sun is already very warm. We are going over to Caledon from Hermanus for it is the great flower place (wild I think, or perhaps it's gardens, I'm not sure) place down here. Here's Dad come back & howling for me – am I ready? – Am I ever ready? (My bag is packed for once) so I must scuttle off.

lots of love from Clyde

A few days later he wrote:

Oct 18th 1938

HMS Amphion
Africa Station

Dear Mummy,

Dad and I have just returned from the most wonderful weekend at Hermanus – marvellous air – vi-spring beds – v good food and surf bathing. I shall really be quite sorry to leave Africa now. I am as brown as a berry (I only hope it won't wear off before we get back! – I feel that "straight from the darkest continent" one should look the part!

...Last night the C in C gave an informal dance for us, which was really great fun. We used a radiogram for music; you know I'm certain that's the best if you can't get a really good band – piano & two squeaky violins not much good. Chipolatas are all the thing out here now – when was it you

first had them!? This country is about ten years behind all the way. This will be my last Epistle from South Africa – I'm sorry to leave, now that departure is imminent, but England has its compensations!

lots of love, from Clyde

On his way home he wrote:

Nov 28th 1938

DAKAR

Madame Anthony Morse,

Dear Mummy,

Here we are at Dakar, my last place in Africa – this afternoon we say goodbye to Dad and the Admiral. I am lunching with Dad and so I'm afraid must write this very quickly. I had a wonderful day yesterday. We rode from seven in the morning until eleven and enjoyed it immensely. In the afternoon I went flying at the civil (Air France) aerodrome and piloted an aeroplane for about two minutes!! It was great fun. We did not stunt or do anything peculiar – just up and down and turning and banking – it really is incredible to look down and see all the things hundreds of feet below. I should love to fly over the house and one could see, at a glance, just where it is and how it stands compared with the rest of the country. You've no idea how much I look forward to seeing you, and it, in 16 day's time –it is marvellously near.

I am sorry this is so short but I must fly over to "Neptune", as this is my last chance to see Dad for some time – he has been much encumbered with official position, he had to hop around with the Admiral – the French here, or some of them, are a lot of fun and we had the best "at home" we have ever had – my French has all come back to me & I get along like a house on fire.

lots of love from Clyde

The *Amphion* arrived at Portsmouth on 15th December 1938 where she paid off and underwent a long refit before being handed over to the Royal Australian Navy as *HMAS Perth.*

Clyde described their arrival and then his journey to Chute Collis for the first time since it had been built. He wrote to his father describing it in detail.

Chute Collis,
Nr Andover, Wiltshire.
CHUTE STANDEN 234

Dec 16th 1938

Dear Dads,

In the last twenty-four hours I have been miraculously wafted from one world into a completely different, but vaguely familiar, new one.

We came up the Channel in the most glorious sunshine – most unseasonable – but wonderful. There were crowds of people and I had great difficulty in finding Mum. I saw her eventually she arrived in a Rolls! (which the Millers have just acquired). She was looking very well and smart in a plum-coloured tweed suit and was with Daphne (Clyde's girlfriend), *also looking most sparkling (I feel like a fashion reporter). I introduced her to the other wives and families who were there. We left the ship at about half-past twelve and went to the Millers for lunch. After a quick visit to Din and her cottage, we set out for Chute. It was dark when we arrived so I got only a very slight impression of the outside.*

After seeing it all in the next couple days, Clyde, gives a long detailed description of the house inside and out. He concludes:

Down to the right of the house (SW) they have made a "grassy sward" which runs right into the wood under the group of three trees. Mum has planted lots of daffodils there, so it will be a lovely arbour in the spring. Going on down the edge of the wood, we went through a small gate in the park rail and went on down to the tennis court. Around the "home field" (on left of house) we put up a brace of partridges and a hare, which was nice to see. (The pigeons are legion and the rooks likewise, when I have got over the monumental cold, which I now enjoy, they will, I fear, have a thin time).

My leave is up on Jan 1st (we start signals on the 2nd), which is terribly short, still, I'm hoping for lots of weekends. I do hope you can read this as I'm writing rather quickly as the post leaves at five – I've already spent two days writing this so I must speed it on its' way.

With love from Clyde.

Chapter 16

War is declared 1939

"Winston is back"

At the beginning of 1939 the heads of the British Government were feeling happier than ever, they believed that the world was entering 'a Golden Age'. As the new decade came in, the mood was changing. In February 1939, Franco finally won the Spanish Civil War. France and Britain officially recognized his Nationalist government. It seemed that the forces of fascism were winning everywhere. Chamberlain and his ministers were still assuring friends and critics that Germany's economic plight made her incapable of going to war. However, Churchill and Eden, at first accused of warmongering, were gaining support, and backbencher MPs angrily shouted 'Heil Chamberlain' at the Prime Minister when he entered the Commons.

Then came the blow. In March 1939, Hitler broke the Munich Agreement. The German Army invaded the remaining part of Czechoslovakia, thereby gaining Prague and Bohemia, along with its military equipment and munitions factories. Hitler then turned his eyes on Poland, hoping to make an agreement with the Poles. Neville Chamberlain, who felt humiliated by Hitler's perfidy over Munich, suddenly did an about turn in policy. He sent Poland an offer of support against 'any action that threatened Polish independence'; the Poles accepted. Britain, with her only ally France, was quite unable to provide it.

King George VI and Queen Elizabeth had been invited to visit Canada by the Canadian Prime Minister Mackenzie, when he came to London in 1937 for their coronation. Despite the uncertain international situation, and fears that they might get stuck the wrong side of the Atlantic if a war broke out, there was no serious thought that they should not go. It was an important chance to consolidate bonds with a Dominion, and by continuing the journey on to Washington and New York there was the chance to influence American public opinion in favour of supporting England if war broke out. The original plan was that they should go on the *HMS Repulse,* which was prepared for the purpose by the Royal Navy, but in the end the ever-practical King persuaded the Admiralty that it was not a good idea to remove one of the country's most powerful warships from the Home Fleet. It would look to the French as if England was not taking the threat of war seriously. In the end, the Canadian Pacific *Empress of Australia* was to be sent and sailed under the White Ensign with the King himself in command. The *HMS Repulse* was to escort her halfway across the Atlantic and then return. It was a grand occasion and the Queen had had a huge wardrobe prepared for the trip. Clyde witnessed the departure and wrote to his father in South Africa:

8 May 1939
H.M.S Excellent
Portsmouth

Dear Dads,

You are so wonderfully regular with your letters that I am going to make a big effort to do the same – this is No 1 of a bigger, brighter and better series!

I start (appropriately) with a Royal Occasion – the departure of the King and Queen from Portsmouth. A most heavenly South African sort of day, hot and still – a bit too hot in the crowd at the Guildhall where I went to watch them arrive by train and be received by the Mayor, Corporation etc.

The King looked very well and dignified and was not in the least nervous. The Queen and the two Princesses looked most sparkling in light blue. The photographs that I have seen of her do not do her justice at all – she really looked quite beautiful, as well as kind and smiling.

As soon as they had left the Guildhall, I rushed back to my car, which I had left in the Barracks. We drove right round the back of Portsea to avoid the crowds and managed to get to Southsea front in time to see the Empress of Australia pass quite close to us. She looked quite nice and very clean with new white paint. I <u>thought</u> I saw the King and Queen and so did everyone else – most satisfactory, but I'm not certain where they were or which they were. Dear old Repulse was out there, and they fell in behind. I'm afraid they must be feeling very fed up at not being able to go. I think it's an absolute scandal that the greatest sea Power in the world cannot send a ship to take its sovereign to America. I know she's the only ship available to catch the Deutschland – but who's so windy about them anyway?

It's a funny feeling not having the King in the country – just like the headmaster going away for a day or two. One feels a bit lost and also anxious in case one of the under masters should do anything rash, or put restriction upon us that we never had before. Taking myself as average, I'm certain we will always have a King – I would never put such blind faith in a committee or Board of Control – one of them is certain to be (or have the reputation of being) a scoundrel, and faith is immediately broken...

The journey for the King and Queen was not a comfortable one. Once in the mid-Atlantic there was freezing fog, high winds and icebergs. They were brought to a standstill for eight hours near Newfoundland, and they were only able to move two more miles in the next sixteen hours. In view of the fairly recent sinking of the Titanic, it was a harrowing experience. They finally arrived in Quebec on 17th May. In fact the King remarked that he had had a good chance for an unexpected rest, although he would not have *"chosen an ice field surrounded by dense fog in which to have a holiday. But it does seem to be the only place for me to rest nowadays!"*

The visit was tremendously successful and widely reported in the press and newsreels. In Washington they stayed with President Roosevelt in the White House. They were the first King and Queen of England to visit America. The welcome was warm, lavish and at the same time, homely. The American public fell in love with the pretty feminine Queen, in her feathered hats and pastel dresses. On the 22nd June they arrived back in England to an ecstatically enthusiastic welcome by crowds of people, who had been following their journey in newspapers. The first transatlantic commercial mail service, operated by Pan American Airways, had flown photographs of the tour in a thirty-seven-ton flying boat, the *Yankee Clipper,* making two stops en route.

Clyde was training and spending weekends at Chute. Later on in the same letter of 8th May to his father, he demonstrates the feeling at the time amongst most of the population of England:

> *...I went to a Fascist meeting the other night – something told me England would never follow Moseley to Victory! (What about Italy? – who wants a concentration camp? Vat about th' Jews? 'Eil 'itler on the f– Quarterdeck –f–balls!). It was not a very large meeting but I was afraid two sailors would get into trouble as they continually made most vulgar, yet amusing remarks which were quite devastating for the speaker.*
>
> *We touch lightly, very lightly, on politics in our War Course. A first class course, which is conducted by Captain Brocking – (flag-wagger) who says he knows you. I enjoyed*

the first half tremendously and am looking forward to the second fortnight that begins next week. I have thought a lot about what to do after courses and come to the conclusion that MTB (motor torpedo boat) is the thing. I met someone the other day who went straight to one without getting his w/keepers certificate in a big ship. I think it would be a good line as it gives a chance for initiative straight away. I'm not too keen on destroyers – I don't know why – I think I should hate living with only two or three other people only, better to be by oneself. As CO of an MTB one can call on lots of people!

I'm tired – Gunnery is most exhausting, especially Field Training. I follow your movements in the paper & hope you are having a good cruise.

Love from Clyde

Jane and Clyde started to bring their friends down to Chute from London or Oxford, for weekend house parties in the new house. They were both enjoying the London Season and going to debutante dances.

Sir John and Isabel Thornycroft, Jane and Clyde standing with friends being Bright Young Things

Clyde, writing to his father comments on one:

> *May 22nd 1939*
>
> *It has at last become a little warmer and I caught the first fish from the Ebble – quite a nice one of ½ lb or more.*
>
> *I went to a dance on Friday evening with a friend of Doo's – Pat Holland – deb's dance – they are mostly very empty-headed and not much to look at. The great relieving feature for me was strawberries – lots of them and I felt very ill on Saturday as I drove down!*
>
> *I went over to the shoot on Sunday & have come to an agreement with the old keeper and things seem to be quite well in hand. I saw a pair of partridges but nothing else – hardly surprising as everything is growing up and the woods are full of bluebells. Our Hookwood is simply heavenly and smells wonderful.*

At this time Clyde was having some difficulties with his mother and Mary. He was growing up and forming his own values. He was probably partly influenced by my mother Jane, his older and much loved sister who, to put it frankly, was more than irritated by Mary's relationship with their mother. I imagine he was a little more ambivalent since he spent less time at home and was not a woman. But like my mother, he was protective of his father, and probably felt his mother had betrayed him by placing so much confidence in Mary. He had a telling off from his mother, but he probably apologised because later letters between them were friendly and easy. But it must have worried him because wrote to his father hinting that things were not straightforward. My grandfather writes back to him:

31st May 1939

H.M.S.NEPTUNE,
Africa Station

Dear Old Boy

Thank you so much for your long letter. I rather like your idea about going in for MTB's. I think it is a good thing to get command as young as you can and you did well in boats and on Amphion & have had the experience of running a powerboat in Nelson, so you should not have any difficulty in handling one. I will write to the Admiralty if you definitely decide to go in for this & see if I can fix it for you.

You haven't answered my letter about your difficulties with Mum and I'd like you to do so if you can – anything you say will be treated absolutely confidentially but I want to help you if I can.

Just been to Durban for a fortnight – much too strenuous as usual but I managed to get away for 2 nights & go to the Drakensberg mountains which are magnificent but sinister. I very much wanted to look over the other side but was neither fit enough nor had the time to do the climb (the top is over about 10,000 feet & the Hostel is about 5,000). It was marvellously cool & fresh, There were the usual crowd of lovelies at Durban & the chaps got very intrigued, Enid & Rosemary Harding were with me & we had a lot of fun together. Not quite so many official parties this time but quite enough. I did 2 goes of flying & did 3 or 4 landings & 2 take off's – my landings were very poor I am afraid, I tried to get down too quickly and the result was the machine wouldn't sit down, however it *was valuable experience and most interesting. Am not really terribly interested in flying myself but I like to know how it's done. You never know when you might have to.*

All the best wishes Old Boy

Good Hunting Dads.

June was extraordinarily hot in England and the Admiralty gave the Fleet its annual summer leave in July, so that ships could be refitted and ready for exercises in August. England was preparing for war. There were slit trenches in Kensington Gardens and posters everywhere describing how to recognize mustard gas. Hotel and restaurant windows were sandbagged; reservists were called up for two or three weeks training.

Stories of Hitler's persecution of the Jews were becoming common. Eleven thousand living in East Prussia had been told to get out by 20th June, and a further ten thousand Polish Jews given the alternative of leaving at once or being put in concentration camps, the horrors of which were becoming known. But in England life carried on, parties continued and, as can be seen from Clyde's letters, people did not really quite believe there would be a war.

There was still a possibility of an agreement with the Russians, but Chamberlain disliked communism and distrusted Stalin. On 23rd August 1939 Russia made an alliance with Hitler. Von Ribbenthrop flew to Moscow and he and Molotov, Russia's Minister of Foreign Affairs signed the German-Soviet non-aggression pact, agreeing that they would partition Poland between them. For the British, the support of the Americans was becoming more and more urgent. In China, the Japanese tacitly supported by Germany, were blockading the British

Concession two miles outside Peking, which since 1860 had housed the British consul and an American settlement.

At dawn on 1st September 1939 Germany invaded Poland. It was the first time in history a combination of tanks and air forces was used, known from then on as "Blitzkrieg" or lightning war. It was easy. The Germans just rolled their tanks across the flat plains to the wide frontiers of Poland. The Poles had already refused to allow the Russians to help defend them – 'better dead than Red!' The railway was bombed and the famed Polish army and cavalry, however well trained and turned out, were no match for this combined mechanical force; not just this, there was another new weapon of war being used for the first time in history – the Germans were confusing the Polish people by broadcasting false news on the radio.

Neville Chamberlain finally realized he had to declare war on Germany. He called his War Cabinet and offered Winston Churchill the command of the Admiralty.

On Sunday the 3rd September 1939 the British Government declared war on Germany in fulfilment of the guarantee it had given Poland. Six hours later, the French Government more hesitantly, followed the British lead. Australia, New Zealand and India (through the Viceroy) declared war the same day. On the 6th - South Africa declared war and on the 10th - Canada joined in.

The Germans were not ready for a World War and had not expected it. Hitler had hoped to expand his territory without opposition; but neither were the Allies properly prepared.

On September 3rd 1939, the Admiralty sent two signals to the Fleet.

One was:

Immediate.... Special telegram
= TOTAL GERMANY++'

And the other:

= **WINSTON IS BACK** + +

My grandfather, as Captain of *The Neptune*, was in the Atlantic off French Senegal, when he announced to his crew that War had been declared. Clyde's idea of MTB's as a career was put aside, as he was assigned to the *HMS Exeter,* a heavy cruiser under Captain Bell, as part of the South Atlantic Fleet.

Chapter 17

The Sinking of the Graf Spee

"It's a pocket battleship"

On August 22nd 1939, as a newly qualified sub-lieutenant, Clyde's summer leave was cut short. He had to rush down to Chute to fetch his gear and then drive all night to join *HMS Exeter* at Devonport, Plymouth. I knew this because amongst the things my grandmother had kept was a diary of Clyde's. It was brief and to the point, almost like a ships log, but from it I managed to piece together the next part of his story. This was ten days before the Second World War was officially declared but was obviously part of the preparations.

As always, there was a great deal of activity to and fro in the oceans, importing and exporting supplies. It was vital to keep merchant shipping lines open, and equally important to the enemy, to try to destroy them. The Germans had 8-inch-gun *panzerschiff* commerce raiders at large, which were a formidable threat. They were more modern than the British ships and were nicknamed by the British 'pocket-battleships'. *Admiral Graf Spee* and the *Deutschland* were roaming the oceans from the end of August 1939, with the specific task of upsetting Allied merchant shipping. The *Graf Spee* slightly exceeded the 10,000-ton restriction of the Versailles Treaty, and was armed with six 11-inch and eight 5.9-inch guns, torpedoes and a floatplane. She had unusually large diesel engines, was very fast and could outgun anything that could catch up with her. She had the advantage that she was one of the few ships, if not the only one at the beginning of the War, that had radar. Both she and the *Deutschland* vanished into the southern Atlantic and Indian oceans, and for four months harried merchant shipping, sinking nine ships in positions as far apart as Brazil and Mozambique. In response, during this time that was called the 'Phoney War', the British and French Navies formed eight hunting groups spread thinly, as far afield as Ceylon and the West Indies; using all the available aircraft carriers, supported by battleships, battle-cruisers and cruisers to search out the *panzerschiff.* The Allies formed groups of two or more ships with the hope they would catch and destroy these pocket-battleships. They were never sure how many ships they were chasing although in fact, unknown to them, the *Deutschland* had returned to Germany and Northern waters quite early on.

Clyde was assigned to part of Force G, one of these hunting groups. They were four ships covering the east coast of South America and the merchant shipping leaving the River Plate and Rio de Janeiro. Commodore Harwood, flying his flag on board *HMS Ajax* a 6-inch cruiser, was in command. Clyde was aboard *HMS Exeter* an 8-inch cruiser under Captain Bell. There was a second 8-inch cruiser *Cumberland,* and another 6-inch cruiser *HMNZS Achilles* commanded by Captain Parry, with a New Zealand crew.

From naval records and telegrams that had been saved, I realized my grandfather was allotted to the same task from South Africa. I imagined him thinking of Clyde and recalling his own first wartime journey at the beginning of World War 1, when he had been a raw Lieutenant in the Dardanelles, hunting the *Goeben* in 1914. This hunt for the pocket battleship was a similar pursuit, only on a much larger scale.

By 25th August Clyde noted in his diary that he was at sea, in convoy with *Colombo* and *Dauntless.* By the 28th he reported that they were in Cape Verde Islands (off Senegal) a convenient place in mid-

Atlantic for supplies. The *Exeter* then left the convoy off St Vincent to meet up with the *Neptune,* his father's ship coming up from South Africa. From 24th–30th September they both thought they were looking for the *Admiral Scheer*, another pocket battleship in the Atlantic. By 3rd October the *Exeter* joined *Ajax, Hotspur, Havock* and *Cumberland* and were still looking for the *Admiral Scheer,* which Clyde records in his diary had been sighted. Unknown to them all on the hunt, *Admiral Scheer* had returned to Germany for an overhaul, after being hit by bombs, and it was, in fact, the *Graf Spee.* At this stage in the war few of the ships had the advantage of radar and were chasing boats by sight or radio communication. The *Graf Spee* had become the terror of the British merchant marines by making lightning strikes across the Atlantic, claiming a victim and vanishing into the huge trackless oceans without a trace, or appearing suddenly in the Indian Ocean. Her daring and imaginative captain, Commander Hans Langsdorff was a Prussian, with a high degree of personal integrity. He captured nine merchant ships and never lost a single man. He was 'old navy' and was said never to have given the Nazi salute, although he defended his country. He thought up various camouflages – making false towers, the crew wearing fake uniforms, changing her name and using a false flag – so the Allies were not sure how many ships they were tracking.

For example, on September 30th the *Graf Spee* sank a 5,000-ton British liner *Clement.* The Germans adhered to 1856 'prize rules', requiring raiders to stop and search ships for contraband and to ensure that their crews were safely evacuated before sinking them. The crew were taken off and South American coast guards told to pick them up, so no lives were lost. On Oct 10th she captured the British freighter *Ashlea,* homeward bound from South America with a precious cargo of 7,000 tons of sugar. The Germans transferred the crew to the *Newton Beach* and appropriated her wireless equipment, sending confusing

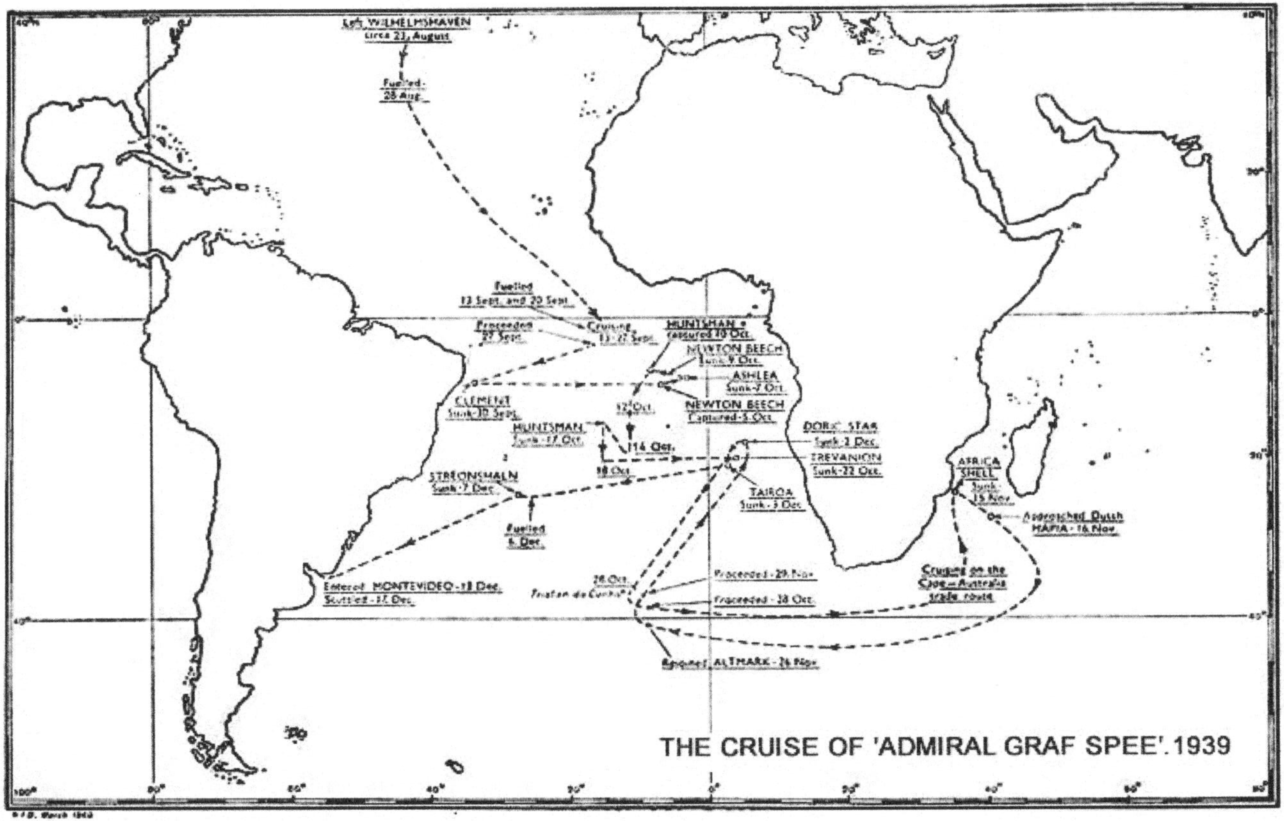
Left WILHELMSHAVEN circa 21 August
Fuelled 28 Aug.
Fuelled 13 Sept. and 20 Sept.
Cruising 13-27 Sept.
Proceeded 27 Sept.
HUNTSMAN captured 10 Oct.
NEWTON BEECH Sunk 9 Oct.
ASHLEA Sunk 7 Oct.
NEWTON BEECH Captured 5 Oct.
CLEMENT Sunk 30 Sept.
HUNTSMAN Sunk 17 Oct.
14 Oct.
18 Oct.
DORIC STAR Sunk 2 Dec.
TREVANION Sunk 22 Oct.
TAIROA Sunk 3 Dec.
STREONSHALH Sunk 7 Dec.
Fuelled 6 Dec.
AFRICA SHELL Sunk 15 Nov.
Approached Dutch HAMIA 16 Nov.
Cruising on the Cape–Australia trade route
Entered MONTEVIDEO 13 Dec. Scuttled 17 Dec.
28 Oct.
Tristan da Cunha
Proceeded 29 Nov.
Proceeded 28 Oct.
Rejoined ALTMARK 26 Nov.
THE CRUISE OF 'ADMIRAL GRAF SPEE'. 1939

signals to the Allied ships in the area, obviously some of which Clyde's Force G was getting. Then the *Newton Beach* was scuttled and the crew transferred to the *Graf Spee.* Shortly after this, another merchant ship, the *Huntsman,* was captured with a mixed cargo of tea, hides, carpets and tropical clothing.

Her crew was transferred to the German *Altmark,* which appeared on the scene disguised as a Norwegian ship, and they were kept prisoners in very hot and difficult conditions until they returned to Germany months later. The *Graf Spee* meanwhile steamed away with her booty. On October 17th the British merchant ship *Trevanion,* alone in mid-Atlantic ocean with a cargo of iron ore, was approached by what she thought was a French ship. She thankfully drew closer to the ship, which immediately hoisted a German flag and signalled her: "stop using your radio or I open fire". It was the *Graf Spee* again, who came nearer and opened fire, torpedoing the *Trevanion* and then took off and disappeared. The *Trevanion* did manage to send a radio message to the Admiralty in London before she sank, and it was my grandfather, commanding *Neptune* operating from South Africa, who was ordered to look for her. They had no luck and eventually heard that she had been torpedoed.

The crews of Force G, Clyde's group, were of course not aware of this activity somewhere out in the ocean, until they received messages through London. They were often bored, chafing from the frustration of being recalled from eight weeks leave and sent to the South Atlantic. Life on board could be very monotonous, especially if you did not have the slightly more comfortable accommodation of the officer class. A steel ship in the tropics was very hot below deck, the spaces in between the machinery resembled a Turkish bath and the crew dripped with sweat all the time, losing weight rapidly. Anything that relieved the boredom, like a school of whales or dolphins, would draw a crowd on deck. A lone whale could look like a submarine and sometimes caused a flurry of excitement. Occasionally, a wandering albatross would hitch a ride on the ship. Morale was often low; especially when they could not go into a port and ran out of fresh vegetables or fruit, or supplies of cigarettes and tobacco. They invented a favourite drink of limejuice sprinkled with raw oatmeal, which was sustaining and cooling. I saw from the brief entries in Clyde's diary that onshore dances and tombola's were sometimes arranged to amuse them.

Tucked into the diary there was a poem Clyde had obviously written to while away the idle hours. He was not Rupert Brooke, but the poem does give a feel of how it was, and it is moving for me to hear the voice of the uncle I never met.

This is a typical, topical, tropical rhyme,
Merely composed for wasting time
When I'm on the bridge and no place to go,
With the blue sky above and the blue sea below,
I don't pace about, with a glass to my eye,
For there's nothing to see, but the sea and the sky,
I haven't learnt knitting, and never could sew
So I hum to myself, "Blue, blah, blow".

When the sun beats down – it's too hot to think,
You pray for Heaven – (in the shape of a drink),
Your brow is all sweaty, there's no wind at all,
No one to talk to, and nowhere to call.
The fishes are flying, the porpoises jump,
They're cool and happy and hearty and plump,
You feel limp, most dreadfully low, the sure reviver is
"Blue, blah, blow".

The Skipper comes up in a cloud of steam,
A short Old Man, but broad in the beam,

He's fiery in action and sticks to his post,
Though shaped by God for a cooler coast.
"Your course is all wrong – just look at the chart,
It just isn't fit for – an ice-cream cart,
Confound you, see, you indolent lout!!"
Disappears down the hatch in a waterspout.

In times like these,
When it's hard to please,
You're trying so hard,
To play the right card,
Your engine fails, you need a tow
The balm for troubles is:
"Blue, blah, blow."

There were various ways of relieving the boredom and 'Crossing the Line' was one of them. I had no idea what it was until I investigated. I found that it was an ancient Navy tradition, said to date back to the Vikings, who believed that gods and goddesses controlled the elements, and made offerings to pacify them. The ceremony commemorated a sailor's first crossing of the Equator, and was a way of the 'old hands' giving their new shipmates training in managing long rough times at sea. The day before the crossing was called 'Wog Day'. The officers stood aside, and let those of the crew who had never 'crossed the line' – called 'polliwogs' – take over the ship, capture and interrogate any – 'shellbacks' – crew who had already crossed the line. When the ship had crossed the equator the shellbacks took control again. They dressed up for a beauty contest in strange costumes representing King Neptune, his wife Amphitrite, and other sea gods. A mock trial was held amongst the pollywogs who were tied up, and a 'truth serum' of horrible concoctions like cracked eggs mixed with aftershave, was poured over their heads and into their mouths.

They had to undergo various tasks such as wear their clothing inside out; crawl on their hands and knees on the slippery deck while being swatted with short lengths of fire hose; or they were locked in stocks and pelted with mushy fruit. After this, they were lathered with another dreadful concoction, shaved with a wooden razor and ducked backwards into a tank of water. Having survived all this, the pollywog was given a certificate, signed by Neptunus Rex, recording the fact that he had crossed the line and was now a fully-fledged shellback. I found a photo of my usually very smart grandfather dressed up, looking like a chef, but on closer inspection, since he had a three-pronged fork in his hand, he was probably dressed as 'Neptune'. Clyde must have already crossed the line on his way to South Africa earlier in the year, and so was a shellback. It was all good fun and helped to relieve the long and similar days; they laughed and forgot their nerves and homesickness. Another diversion they could look forward to at beginning of December was when they were allowed to take over the galley and mix Christmas puddings.

Anthony 'Crossing the Line'

For a few days 18th-21st October Clyde writes he played deck hockey and there was a tombola. On the 26th he reports that *Achilles* joins them and they make for Montevideo in South America. By Nov 1st they had a dance on what must have been the Falkland Islands, as on Nov 4th Clyde says they left there. On 8th November they had a tombola on board at Mar de Plata, a tourist town south of the River Plate, but Clyde comments:

Lousy, did not get ashore - would have been OK in season.

And on 13th November:

We set out for South Africa and Simonstown, swopping places with the other squadron, but on a report of a big enemy raider (10,000 tons - a pocket battleship) — we turn back so that the others can go off and investigate (probably his father on board *Neptune*).

On Nov 18th his father was ordered back to Cape Town and on the way they intercepted the German passenger ship *Adolph Woermann*, in spite his attempts to stop her, she was scuttled by her own crew, and they had to take on board 162 unexpected passengers, including 25 women and 2 children, and deposit them in Cape Town. I knew this from the congratulatory telegram from the Admiralty that was still amongst my grandmother's collection of letters:

NAVAL MESSAGE

TO: *Cin C.S.A 535® HMS Neptune*

FROM: *Admiralty 19.03 25th November*

Admiralty appreciate energetic steps taken by Commanding officer HMS Neptune to prevent German ship Adolph Woermann sinking herself.

Clyde then writes on 29th November: '*Arrive*'. This must have been to join the others at the River Plate. On 1st December he writes

"Dance" and again on 4th December. On 2nd and 3rd December, unknown to them, but of course recorded in the archives, the *Graf Spee* attacked *Doric Star* and *Tairoa* on their way home round the Cape from Australia and New Zealand, carrying butter, cheese, frozen meat and Christmas turkeys. Both ships managed to scuttle, without letting the Germans get a cargo they would have dearly appreciated, after so long at sea with no fresh supplies. The two ships did, however, succeed in transmitting wireless signals before sinking.

The Admiralty was the only way to coordinate all these movements in the Atlantic and they thought the *Graf Spee* was probably somewhere between Cape Town and Freetown. On Dec 6th they ordered my grandfather and Force K, to do a twelve-day sweep, passing St Helena again. They had no success and found out, only when they were back in Cape Town, that while they sailed south, they had passed *Graf Spee* sailing north, about 750 miles west of them and the island of St Helena.

Clyde's fleet near the River Plate waited. Each day small naval aircraft would take off and scour the seas for a sight of the German ships. Once they were back, the crew would spend most of the night on deck in the cooler air under the stars. So far, the aircraft had not seen anything of the *Graf Spee,* who was remarkably successful in hiding herself. They knew, even with four ships, that they were a poor match, but Commodore Harwood was an experienced and wily sailor who knew South American waters well. He had carefully thought out his tactics if he should encounter her. He was a fair opponent for Langsdorff. On December 11th my grandfather on the *Neptune* was again at the mouth of the River Amazon, very close but he did not see *the Exeter.*

When Commodore Harwood on the *Ajax* received the report of the attack on the *Doric Star* and *Tairoa*, he decided that there were three likely destinations the *Graf Spee* would go for refuelling and supplies – Rio de Janeiro, the Falklands or the River Plate. He reckoned Langsdorff would probably go for the River Plate. The *Exeter*, *Ajax* and *Achilles* therefore waited together at the centre of the shipping routes off the mouth of the River Plate. On the morning of 13th December, the weather was fine and clear, visibility was good and the sea was calm. They were one ship short as the *Cumberland* had gone to the Falklands for a refit. At 06.14 in the morning they sighted smoke to the east. Commodore Harwood had correctly anticipated the *Graf Spee's* movements.

At that tremendous moment they realised that the time they had been expecting had come. Clyde's ship, the *Exeter,* was sent to investigate and signalled Commodore Harwood, on the bridge of the little cruiser *Ajax*: 'It's a pocket battleship!' In four minutes all hands were on deck, even though many sailors were sleeping at the time and they were only at cruising stations. In many ways the crew were relieved to hear the marine bugler's 'Open Fire' and jumped to it with vigour. The *Exeter* got there first. Faced with *Graf Spee's* heavier armament, Harwood's plan had been to split his force in two, and try to divide *Graf Spee's* main guns. They all advanced from different angles in order to confuse the enemy, harrying her from all sides. *Exeter* closed in to the south, while the two light cruisers worked around to the north, firing as they manoeuvred. At 06.17 *Graf Spee* sighted *Exeter,* and closed in on her at full speed, opening fire, thus beginning the Battle of the River Plate.

Exeter's starboard propeller had been damaged in a refuelling operation with a tanker in heavy seas, so range taking at speeds in excess of eighteen knots became progressively inaccurate. However, her 8-inch salvoes struck the *Graf Spee,* and the other cruisers were hitting effectively from the north. Then *Graf Spee* turned and concentrated her two 11-in turrets on *Exeter,* hitting her badly and knocking out B turret, destroying all her communications on the bridge. All those on the bridge were instantly killed or wounded. The steering gear was damaged putting the ship out of control. While Captain Bell was going from the bridge to take over aft, Clyde as Acting Sub-Lieutenant, went from his action station to the Air Defence Officer's position. Seeing no one alive on the bridge, he jumped down and managed to establish communication with the lower conning tower until a senior officer appeared. Then he gave detailed orders for the disposal of the wounded on the flag deck. A fire was burning on the forecastle. He organised a party to deal with it, but realized the group was too small to cope, and so ran aft collecting more hands, and rushed back to the forecastle. Shortly after this a shell exploded there. Clyde was killed and his body blown over the side. He was nineteen years old.

I pursued the sad accounts of Clyde's end. It is a story, which was to affect the lives of my grandparents and my mother so much. I pieced it together from letters sent by the Admiralty to my grandparents, and the official reports published about the Battle of the River Plate. Although I never met Clyde, he felt close and he was 'family'. It happened to many people's sons in a war but it did not make it any less tragic. All the details were faithfully recorded by the officers and shipmates, kept, and later relayed to suffering families. One of the things that struck me, when reading the individual accounts of the uncle who I never knew, was the care the crew had for each other. The letters and Clyde's diary, that had eventually reached me all these years later, were lovingly kept in a small black ship's box with his initials, C.A.L.M. on it – Clyde Anthony Leeds Morse. The small details recorded by shipmates, and the countless letters of condolence formed a part of my history. My grandfather was not someone who kept or hoarded things, he moved around too much, but he saved these. They were from people all over the world who obviously loved and respected him. The heartbreak was that he had just started to know and appreciate his now adult son as a companion and friend. He must have been grateful for that, but that he should have been so swiftly taken away from him was heartrending. He was not given to emotion, but it seemed to me from the replies and subsequent events, that my grandfather retreated further into a solitary place no-one could reach. It was obvious he became determined to do his duty and beat the Germans. He threw himself into his work, which he did well, but family life was never the same again. The accounts by people who served under him showed respect and admiration, but he was obviously remote. He was not, of course, unique. There were many parents who suffered similar losses. It brought home to me, more than anything else could, the pointlessness and tragedy of war, without negating the heroism and nobility of those who fought it.

By 07.40 Captain Bell, who was unhurt, decided that *Exeter* was unable to continue the fight and he steamed away south to the Falklands to repair her. Many of the crew had been killed or wounded. From then on the ship limped southwards, listing badly and on fire. The survivors of the shattering experience thanked God for their lives, and realized that their training – what had previously seemed the boredom of repetitive habits and routine exercises – now kept them functioning, in the confusion and loss of their companions. *Ajax* and *Achilles* continued to harry the *Graf Spee* from the north. At 07.25 *Ajax* lost her two after-turrets and *Achilles* was also damaged. Commodore Harwood decided to break off the fight until dark when he could use his small ships and torpedoes more effectively, and so under the cover of smoke he turned away. It had all taken one hour and twenty minutes.

Although this was the end of Clyde's story, the sequence is interesting because it shows that they had not lost their lives in vain.

Victory came in its own way with the patience of Captain Henry Harwood. The *Graf Spee* had only superficial damage to her guns, but Captain Langsdorff was running out of ammunition and had been at sea for three and a half months. He decided to head for the Uruguayan port of Montevideo, to repair the damage. He made off, the two British cruisers still hanging grimly to his heels like terriers. She entered port at midnight. Montevideo was a neutral port and according to international law, the *Graf Spee* was only allowed to stay 72 hours repairing damage, taking in stores and landing the wounded. The *Ajax* and *Achilles* lay outside the harbour like watchdogs, waiting for her to come out. That night the *Cumberland* rejoined them after steaming at full speed from the Falklands.

Meanwhile, Winston Churchill in London and the British Ambassador in Uruguay, Sir Eugen Millington-Drake, were cooking up a cunning plan to alarm Langsdorff. Churchill sent out an order on the radio to all the available ships, to gather in the area to catch the *Graf Spee* when she emerged from the River Plate. This was largely a bluff, as there were not many more ships available; but it had the effect of scaring Captain Langsdorff, who desperately telegraphed Hitler for instructions. He thought it was impossible to escape to the open seas and back to Germany. First, he tried to extend his stay in Montevideo to longer than the 24-hours he had left. Since that was not possible, on the afternoon of 17th December the *Graf Spee* transferred more than 700 men, baggage and provisions to a German merchant ship in the harbour. At 6.15 pm as the sun was beginning to set, watched by immense crowds curious to see what would happen, the *Graf Spee* left harbour and steamed slowly out to sea, awaited by the British cruisers at the mouth of the River Plate. No one was quite sure what would take place. When the ship was about three miles out to sea, there was some activity with two tugs. Then at 8.45 pm, as the sun was just going down behind the horizon, there was a huge explosion and smoke billowed up. *Graf Spee* was at her end. Commodore Harwood said:

> "It was dark and she was ablaze from end to end, flames reaching almost as high as the control tower, a magnificent and most cheering sight."

The irony was that on that day, my grandfather was up in Rio refuelling, but had not gone ashore. He had refuelled, and on 18th December headed back south, and heard nothing until later.

Captain Langsdorff disappeared, amongst rumours that he had gone up in the ship, but then on 20th December it was heard he had shot himself in his hotel room in Buenos Aires. Although his actions had been authorised by Hitler, he felt heartbroken at the loss of his ship and could not bear the humiliation. The letter he left to the German Ambassador in Buenos Aires was as follows:

> Dec. 19, 1939
>
> Your Excellency,
>
> After a long struggle I reached the grave decision to scuttle the Admiral Graf Spee, in order to prevent her from falling into enemy hands. I am still convinced that under the circumstances this decision was the only one left, once I had taken my ship into the trap of Montevideo...Sooner than expose my ship to the danger that after a brave fight she would fall into enemy hands, I decided not to fight but to destroy the equipment and then scuttle the ship. It was clear to me that this decision might be unwittingly misconstrued, by persons ignorant of my motives, as being attributable to personal considerations. Therefore I decided from the beginning to bear the consequences involved in this decision. For a captain with a sense of honour, it goes without saying that his personal fate cannot be separated from that of

his ship. I postponed my intention as long as I still bore responsibility for decisions concerning the welfare of the crew under my command. After today's decision of the Argentine government, I can do no more for my ship's company. Neither will I be able to take an active part in the present struggle of my country. I can now only prove by my death that the fighting services of the Third Reich are ready to die for the honour of the flag. I alone bear the responsibility for scuttling the Admiral Graf Spee. I shall face my fate with firm faith in the cause and the future of the nation and of my Führer. I am writing this letter to Your Excellency in the quiet of the evening, after a calm deliberation, in order that you may be able to inform my superior officers, and to counter public rumors if this should become necessary.

Kapitän zur See Hans Langsdorff

In England, the sinking of the *Graf Spee* and the exploits of the brave little ships *Exeter, Ajax* and *Achilles,* was hailed as a victory for the Allies. The news was full of bravery and heroism and it brightened the dreary cold winter at the beginning of the War. For almost a year after that, the Atlantic was relatively free of trouble from commerce-raiders, and so the losses incurred were not without success. Eventually when the *Exeter* limped back to Plymouth, one of the survivors wrote:

> "We mourned our losses and felt for those near to them, but the need for hard work necessary to the return of trained men to the war effort was welcomed, and eventually, with an escort that grew as we approached these shores, we entered Plymouth Sound to be greeted by crowds who had found relief from their 'phoney war' in the news of our action."

For Anthony and Marly at separate ends of the earth, the devastating news of Clyde's death reached them by telegram, those telegrams dreaded by the parents of people in the Armed Services. Then letters of condolence and appreciation of Clyde's qualities poured in. But they could not bring him back.

Chapter 18

England 1940

"...blood, toil, tears and sweat"
Churchill

The winter of 1939/40 in England was the coldest for forty-five years. There were drifts of snow on the Wiltshire Downs and it showed no sign of shifting. Farmers were forced to keep sheep and cattle in sheds, and winter food stores were running out. Letters from Chute complained that they were without electricity for several days making everything more difficult. They rattled around in the big house that had built for so many guests; now it was just the three of them. The chauffeur-cum-gardener, Yorke, had joined up so it fell to Mary to chop the firewood.

Nan spent a lot of time trying to keep at least one room in the house warm. They became conscious of fuel and food running out, and started to save things in case of scarcity. They huddled together in the drawing room, or better still in Nan's small sitting room, which warmed up quicker and was less wasteful. Mary and Nan were great knitters so they made socks and scarves to be sent off to the soldiers. They delayed going up to bed until their hefty ceramic hot water bottles had time to heat through the cold linen sheets, blankets and eiderdowns, often undressing in front of the fire and then running up quickly into a warm bed. Putting out pieces of fat and fresh water for the squabbling bluetits outside the kitchen window was easy, but shovelling snow was back breaking and seemed very arduous. Somehow this cold and this winter were not the same as others. The news of troops, desperately fighting in Europe in freezing conditions, filtered through on the wireless. They were not too worried about Clyde and Anthony patrolling the Atlantic; they had none of the details and were proud they were doing their duty.

Then the fateful telegram arrived at Chute addressed to my grandfather and written in pencil by the postmaster at Chute. My grandmother received it, as he was far away in South Africa.

POST OFFICE

TELEGRAM

From Admiralty — **Time handed in** 1939

Capt J A V Morse Chute Collis Nr Andover Wilts from Admiralty

Deeply regret to inform you that your son, Acting Sub Lieutenant Clyde A.L Morse, Royal Navy is reported as missing believed killed in action December 13th.

It was a tremendous shock. There followed a letter from the Admiralty:

Mrs J.A.V Morse,
Chute Collis 18th December 1939

Madam

In confirmation of the Admiralty's telegram of 17th December, I am commanded by My Lords Commissioners of the Admiralty to state that they have learnt that your son, Sub-Lieutenant Clyde Anthony Leeds Morse, Royal Navy, is missing and believed to have been killed in the action of 13th December between His Majesty's Ships EXETER, AJAX and ACHILLES and the German Warship GRAF SPEE.

My Lords desire me to express to you their regret at receiving this intelligence and their deep sorrow that this victory should have entailed so great a loss to you.

I am, Madam,
Your obedient Servant,
R.H. Marten

Then written by hand: -

"A very gallant lad, of whom you must feel very proud".
G.H.D'O Lyon,
Vice Admiral
Commander-in-Chief

For my grandmother the news was unexpected and devastating. Her son, who so little time ago had been there at Chute Collis, planning the garden and finishing off of the house, was gone. Forever. He was never coming back.

Her memoirs came to a halt. I realized that probably her grief dampened her desire to describe her life. Now I had to piece the story together, between the photograph albums, the letters that she had kept, and contemporary accounts of the events of the War. It left me with many reflections about my grandparent's lives and the influences I could now see in my own character. It was only five years before I was born. I saw from their story that I had been affected by this loss and pain that broke the family, as a result of the War. At the same time, I believe it was part of my destiny and that of my whole generation.

At first everyone rallied round and kept Marly afloat. Her sister Din and Aunt San Cameron came to visit for Christmas and then again in February. The weather made it difficult for them to come often, as everyone was snowed in and people were ill with flu. Din wrote that she was busy doing duty at a First Aid Post and complaining that her maid had taken off to marry a sailor with only four days notice. She was unable to leave San alone in the house, and had to keep house on her own, something unthought-of for most of her class until after the War. Din was my great aunt and never married, but she had been my favourite relation.

Din (left) on board Neptune in 1937

I remember her as a practical and industrious woman who loved her garden, wild birds and her poodle Percy. Her childlike innocence made her sympathetic to a young girl, and as I grew up she taught me to love country ways and animals; to adults, especially her own sister Marly, Din often seemed naive and irritating.

My grandmother, after the initial shock, seemed to go through a period of fury with the Admiralty. She wrote to them complaining she had received not one telegram, but three. She worried about salvaging what there was of Clyde's belongings. She must have felt they were some part of him she could hold on to and touch. Almost sixty years later, I was grateful for her insistence, because from those few possessions, mostly letters, I could piece together the story. There were patient and polite replies from the Admiralty doing their best to soothe her. As it was the early days of the War there were not as many casualties as later on, but she cannot have been the only distraught mother.

A telegram arrived from my grandfather, busy serving in the Atlantic and not able to come back. It was the fastest form of communication in those days, when letters took a long time to come by ship, and at sea even sending one was sometimes a difficult.

POST OFFICE

TELEGRAM

From Sans Origine **Time handed in** EE

12.20 28 23rd December 1939

Andover Post Office Hants

GLT MORSE CHUTE COLLIS ANDOVER ENG

D

WISH I COULD BE WITH YOU TO HELP MY LOVE AND SYMPATHY TO YOU FAMILY AND NAN = ANTHONY MORSE + +

It must have seemed small consolation and probably she felt, somewhat unreasonably, that he could have come to comfort her, although she knew she was the wife of an officer in the Armed Services, at War. Of course in times of extreme grief, one is often not logical. Anyway almost certainly, having grown up amongst women, she found it easier to express her grief to another woman. In this case it was Mary. The letters of condolence poured in and needed to be answered. Mary coped with most of the correspondence and forwarded things on to Anthony in South Africa, writing on each letter neat little notes as to her reply. Jane came down to Chute but, after the initial shock, she stayed away in Oxford. She was busy and had her own life;

her relationship with her mother had never been easy. There was a heavy Victorian cloud of grief over the house that she could not bear. Suddenly everything Clyde had done was idolized and held in comparison with her own shortcomings, and she had her own grief over the death of her brother whom she loved very much. I realized my mother probably felt left very alone. Mary was holding the fort and looking after her mother who had gone to pieces; she had long occupied the space in her mother's heart that perhaps she might have held, but it was too late.

A letter from Anthony's sister Enid arrived from South Africa, where she was still visiting Anthony and friends:

Admiral's Office
Simonstown

Jan: 8. 1940

Dearest Marly

I can only send my loving sympathy. Somehow this has been worse than anything in the last war because then one was young and willing oneself to die for an ideal.

But now with the experience of life behind one, to think that lovely lives like his darling Clyde should be given that we may live just makes me crazy. Enid

Anthony with Enid on Neptune

This War was not looking hopeful for the Allies, although the success of the Battle of the River Plate, and the heroism of Clyde and his shipmates on the *Exeter*, had been hailed as a bright spark of hope in that dreary winter. While Marly, Mary and Nan were freezing at Chute, the Germans occupied Norway and Denmark, and the Russians invaded Finland. At the beginning of May, bowing to general concern that he could not lead the country at war, Neville Chamberlain resigned and Winston Churchill became Prime Minster. The same week, Hitler's Panzer divisions burst through Holland, Belgium and northern France on their way to the Channel coast. Anthony Eden, now British Secretary of State for War, hurriedly sent out the British Expeditionary Force (BEF) led by Lord Gort, a grenadier from the First World War. This consisted of as many tanks as they could ship over the Channel, a considerable manoeuvre in itself, supported by Bomber Command. It was familiar terrain for the Army – the Somme, Agincourt and Waterloo had all been fought there – but this time the leaders were out of date. They were planning defensive strategy in terms of traditional infantry regiments, trusting in the English Channel and the Navy to protect the British Isles. It had more or less worked in the First World War, notwithstanding huge losses of men fighting in the trenches. The Allied (British, French, Dutch and Belgian) numbers were greater than the German, but they were taken by surprise at the speed and organization of the German offensive. Dubbed 'Blitzkrieg' (lightning war) and first used against the Poles, the combined Panzer divisions of fast moving tanks, motorbikes and infantry with dive-bombing Luftwaffe, threw the Allies into panic. It seemed to the foot soldiers as if there were planes, tanks and men everywhere. The attacks were well co-ordinated and used radio communication between tanks. Hitler's commanders were young and modern, people like General Guderian, Chief of Mobile Forces (nicknamed '*Schneller Heinz* - Hurrying

Heinz'), a pioneer of armoured warfare; and the daring intuitive Major General Erwin Rommel, who later became famous as 'The Desert Fox', when fighting with his *Africakorps* against Montgomery in North Africa. Even Hitler and the more traditional German High Command were surprised at the mayhem caused by this combination of speed and audacity. It was a type of warfare that no one had ever previously experienced. The BEF were driven back to the coast, unable to halt the onslaught, and the only solution was to 'get out quick'. Guderian was only halted from destroying all the Allied forces by orders from his nervous High Command.

On 26th May Churchill ordered 'Operation Dynamo', the 'Miracle escape at Dunkirk'. He instructed the Navy, and as many of the little ships that England could muster, to cross the channel and bring home the troops. Dunkirk was an emotional and inspiring episode, of 'little' England with her 'back against the wall' holding her own against the terrifying forces of the Germans, using her famous English Channel to protect her from European invasion. This 'Spirit of Dunkirk' I recognized from my childhood, as the same spirit that helped the English survive the Blitz the following year – a cheerful no-nonsense pulling together and refusal to be intimidated in adversity. It was a part of British character and 'backbone' that had been admired throughout the world and had built the Empire.

Churchill used the opportunity to make stirring and very effective speeches, encouraging Commonwealth solidarity in the face of the hard times ahead. At Chute, like the rest of the world, they tuned in to the wireless and listened to the broadcasts by the BBC, inspiring the Allied Forces; first hearing Big Ben chiming and then the famous: "This is London..." I remember my grandmother's admiration of Churchill as a war leader. His extraordinary gift of oratory stirred the fighting spirit of British Empire to beat the 'Bosch or Jerry's', as they were commonly called, even though at the beginning of the War, it seemed the Allies had little hope:

> "We are in the preliminary stage of one of the greatest battles in history... we are in action at many points — in Norway and in Holland — we have to be prepared in the Mediterranean… the air battle is continuous, and many preparations have to be made here at home. I would say to the House as I said to those who have joined this government: **I have nothing to offer but blood, toil, tears and sweat**. We have before us an ordeal of the most grievous kind. We have before us many, many long months of struggle and of suffering. You ask, what is our aim? I can answer in one word: Victory. Victory at all costs — Victory in spite of all terror — Victory, however long and hard the road may be, for without victory there is no survival."

His rhetoric was a fair match for Hitler's, which had so successfully inspired the Germans into action.

The Isle of Wight Ferry, *Fishbourne,* which my grandmother knew from so many trips across to Ryde, was amongst the little boats that went out to Dunkirk. She must have remembered her time on the 'Bum Boat' in the previous war, helping the sailors in the Solent. Most of the men were evacuated but a lot of equipment was lost, abandoned in the hurry to save human lives. The debacle was viewed by those leaving France as 'a scene filled with a sense of finality and death, the curtain ringing down on a great tragedy.' The troops arriving in Dover, however, painted a different picture. It was reported in the newspapers:

> "Unwashed, unshaven in our rags and tatters, we were welcomed by people from all walks of life; those at the top of the league were the crew who brought us back, the medical men who attended the sick and wounded, and the Women's Voluntary Service who gave every man a mug of tea, a piece of cake and a cigarette. After we settled down in the waiting train a soldier got to his feet and said, 'Boys, I'm thanking God I'm home. Now let us give a thought to the boys we left behind.' And we all stood in silence in that compartment as we travelled through the green fields, and I thought England wasn't such a bad place after all."

The snow finally melted and spring came late. At Chute Collis, the big handsome house that had only just been finished before the outbreak of War echoed in its emptiness. It had been designed for the family before the War, with the idea of a life of ease and enjoyment. Now it was filled with a deep sadness.

Chute Collis newly built

Chapter 19

Anthony 1939-40

On December 19th my grandfather was at sea in command of *Neptune* in the Atlantic, on his way south again, when the report about Clyde was telegraphed through to the ship. The crew were instructed not to discuss the news. He was very brave and showed nothing. Stiff upper lip, but more than that, he was a man who had never shared his feelings with anyone, a private man in command of a ship in the middle of a War that was going badly. He could not give in to emotion. On the 20th the news about Captain Hans Langsdorff's suicide came through. When they berthed in Freetown on Boxing Day, a fellow officer took him ashore for lunch, and as it was very hot, a swim, and tried to keep him cheerful, but it must have been the most tremendous blow. For him it was a sad twist of fate that it was his son, who was beginning his life, who had encountered the Graf Spee, when it could have so easily been himself.

Gradually the letters of sympathy and condolence filtered through the various ships' P.O boxes where he could collect them, and like my grandmother, he saved them. The letters came from far and wide, from officers serving all over the world, fighting in a War which was no longer a "Phoney War" but very real. There were many from fellow officers in the Navy, he was well known and well loved.

Clyde's captain wrote:

H.M.S Exeter
28th December 1939

My dear Morse,

I know that words are idle but my thoughts have been long with you in our tragic loss. I offer you my deepest and heartfelt sympathy.

Your boy was a great lad and if it is any comfort to you may I say that he met his end in the finest traditions of the Service.

I think Jennings has told you, he displayed great initiative when the bridge had been swept by eleven-inch splinters, and then, regardless of any personal danger, with the utmost coolness and promptitude, and again with initiative not often found in one so young, he proceeded to the forecastle with the intention of putting out a fire there. Poor lad he was never seen again, another eleven inch bursting there just when he arrived.

If it is any consolation it is safe to say he knew nothing about it.

I know this letter is poor recompense to you but I wanted you to know how much we all admired and mourn him.

With my deepest sympathy
Very sincerely
Fred. S. Bell.

The ship's chaplain of the *HMS Ark Royal*, an aircraft carrier that had not quite made it to the Battle of the River Plate, also wrote:

H.M.S Ark Royal
Dec 26th1939

Dear Old Friend,

I had in mind to visit you, but, on second thoughts, beg leave to send you a little letter instead.

Not that I can express all I feel any better that way, but that I hope it is easier for you to bear with my intrusion, in writing. To have served as long as you and I have, in sight of one another, is a strong tie between us. To have watched each other's family grow up is stronger still. But strongest of all is to stand beside you at this overwhelming hour of affliction and of pride.

And believe me, John Anthony, that is where I do place myself just now, and I don't only stand, I kneel as well. And when the first days of loss are past, and you two who must so desperately need each other now, are together again, just speak of my sympathy to the little Mother, will you? Do not think of me as missing the agony of it all, on the very fringe of the operation and longing to be there, "would God I had died for thee." I have Anthony too, just left Freetown in escort to a convoy. How far are we apart, you and I, at such a time as this?

There is a poem which I long to pass to you later on, if it would not seem a trespass Just as the two generations put their heads together sometimes over a home problem, and the older believes he can show the way, but the younger gets there first sees the point in a flash even so in other ways the leadership falls into the younger hands and the little child does lead.

The whole of our Faith is centred around the sacrifice of a beloved son – the keystone of our Universe – it looked like loss, but meant the safety of the Human race and from this Calvary of yours and from other gifts, so freely given, will spring the virtue and strength and remembrance of the new England that is to be, when this job is done. So be of good courage, J A and the Lord He very gracious to you both "in sure and certain Hope." And he said "Fight on, fight on."

Yours ever

JWB Moore

From another officer on board the *Ark Royal* who had known Clyde:

H.M.S Ark Royal

29/12/39

Dear Captain Morse,

I was indeed sorry to hear that you had lost Clyde in the action with the Graf Spee. I got to know him pretty well during his time in Amphion and soon saw that he was a very capable young officer, and I am quite certain that he did his duty in that splendid fight with courage and efficiency.

But what struck me most about Clyde was his outstanding personality. He was so eagerly interested in life in general and was always ready to take part, with distinction, in anything that was going on. In addition he was perfectly content to keep his own company and make his own interests and amusements, a rare quality in these days.

Yours Sincerely

George Beale

From these letters one can see that the Navy looked after each other like a family; they watched over each other's sons, who were coming up through the ranks. They moved around ships and commands and because they were away at sea together, sometimes for many months, they were often closer than the family back home. They shared the same experiences and saw each other through the difficult and good times, especially when they were at war. There were many from South African officers, colleagues and friends. Admiral Charles Stuart from Admiralty House, Simonstown and his wife, with whom he and Enid had become great friends, wrote with much caring sympathy. His old friend, Rear Admiral Gerald Dickens, Charles Dickens's grandson, whom he had known since the Dardanelles, and who had introduced him to Marly, wrote:

ADMIRALTY

22.1.40

My dear old Antonio

I've only just heard the news that must have blotted out the sun for you. I missed the list of Exeter casualties & only heard it second hand & Tony wasn't mentioned. Now by chance I've heard of that splendid boys death. Believe me Antonio your old and very affectionate friend is moved more deeply than he can express at the thought of your grief. What a loss. Any son would be, but yours was so exceptional in charm, gaiety (his intense *joie de vivre* makes his death at that age so particularly cruel) and as a promising young officer. The only thing of comfort you can bite on is that he died in a victorious action. Pearl will be so distressed when I tell her. We often spoke of him when talking of you - as we often do & we've often said how fitting it was that such a fine father should have such a fine son.

Alas nothing I can say will help you, but I must write this line to tell you how deeply I am moved & how deeply I sympathise. God bless you old chap.

Yrs Always Dick

P.S. Off in a fortnight as N.A. (naval attaché) Hague & Brussels

The Governor of Sierra Leone, Sir Douglas James Jardine OBE wrote:

GOVERNMENT HOUSE,
SIERRA LEONE.
28 December 1939

Dear Morse,

I feel I must write a line to tell you how very sad I have felt since I heard of your grievous loss. I can only hope that your own personal sorrow is lessened in some measure by the knowledge that your son died as every good Britisher would wish to die fighting against great odds for what he knows to be right. But, at the best, that can only be consolation for you as a Captain R.N., and I know that as a father you find it much more difficult to reconcile yourself to what the Fates have decreed.

Forgive an ill-expressed letter, which brings all the sympathy, which I find impossible to put into writing.

Yours v. sincerely Douglas Jardine

The following one reached him only in March, from their old friend Denis Orr, who was attached to Sudan Defence Force, the Army in Sudan:

EASTERN ARAB CORPS,
GEDAREF,
SUDAN.
28.1.40

Dear Anthony & Marly

I was most terribly sorry to hear of Clyde's death in the 'Exeter' and my deepest sympathy goes to you both. He was such a 'ripper'. If there is any consolation, then it must to know that he was killed putting up a most magnificent show. I do hope, Marl, that you have got Anthony with you, but I fear that he may still be in South Africa. I will say no more as anything that I did say would be inadequate; I think you will understand my feelings.

My love to you both
Yours ever
Denis Orr

There were cards in French from fellow officers in the French Navy in Force X, who had also been chasing the *Graf Spee,* and knew Clyde and my grandfather from this time in the Atlantic. One of them, Commandant Jaques Trolley Prevaux, had been in Shanghai at the same time as Anthony. He was a heroic, brave and very romantic figure, who had received a Croix de Guerre in the First World War. Later in this War, he went on to become an Admiral and receive the Croix de Guerre a second time, when he fought in the French Resistance. He was finally tortured and shot by the Gestapo in 1944. He died alongside his second wife, and their surviving daughter published a book called 'Jaques and Lotka. Love in the Tempest of History', telling the story. Another was from Vice-Amiral Duplat from Force X on board *Dupleix*, appreciating Clyde's qualities. Both were based in Dakar under British Vice-Admiral G H D'O Lyon, Commander-in-Chief Africa Station.

Then there were those from the family. Perhaps one of the most dear and moving was from Nan who had been like a mother to Clyde and Jane. My mother said she loved Nan as the only mother she had. She writes on her own rather sweet monogrammed notepaper, headed NAN in red embossed letters, a moving slightly misspelt letter; her only education had been what she had picked up from their family as she had gone to live with Marly's mother at a very young age.

Nan

Chute Collis
Jan 14th

Dear Sir

I am very grieved about our dear Tony. I can't put into words how I feel for you & Mrs Morse, she is a very brave woman, because it must hurt very much, when she is answering all the letters, she has received. I have tried to write to you several times but some how it was very difficult, it is very hard to relise that he will never return, we are so use to you both being away. I wish you were here, is there any possible chance of you getting leave. I received a letter from you yesterday & I thank you very much for your comforting words.

I am knitting sea boot stockings for the navy and I would like to send them to you to give to one of the men. I will ask Mrs Morse advise & send them when they are finished.

Now dear Sir I wish I could help you & Mrs Morse in your great loss, but I am afraid no one can do that, only god's blessing to help and comford you I hope you are keeping well

I am yours
Sincerely Nan

Nan in her Nurse's uniform

Marly's Aunt San Cameron wrote:

San in her Red Cross uniform

Dec 20th '39

My dearest Anthony,

I know you well enough to guess what this blow will be to you but also that you will be proud of your son that he lost his life in such a gallant fight He is a lovely memory for us and we mustn't begrudge him his passing into the great Beyond…I have a strong conviction that Clyde won't be lonely over the other side. Gags (Marly's mother) and Maurice (San's husband) will help him at first. Is that old fashioned of me? Never mind it's a good thought. What a marvellous Naval Battle it was and how proud we all are of "Exeter" – She was wonderful.

We hope to meet again at Din's on Christmas day – but only if Marl feels like it and if Jane would like it. But I think it is best to try to be together if we can. We shall think of you so much. All my love and prayers are with you –

Yours ever, San

Din will miss Clyde dreadfully – he was everything to her

Din was indeed very sad; she loved Clyde who had so appreciated her love of the countryside and birds.

She wrote:

Pinetrees Cottage,
Fareham

Dec 22nd
Darling Anthony,
I know so well how stricken you must be by this terrible blow that has fallen on us all…
Half the reason for the building of this little cottage is now gone, but I shall still remember thankfully this last summer which was made so much more happy for me by Clyde's frequent visits and companionship & interest in my small garden– he did so many little jobs for me & in his most charming last letter asked with much interest about the various doings in my garden – I have been planting lots of roses and young trees & was so looking forward to his inspection of them in the spring.
I have a good deal to see to here & work at 1st Aid Post – which is a help – Darling Anthony, all my love & sympathy go out to you but I know how proud you must be of him. much, much love from a sorrowful Din.

In January a long letter arrived from Mary, which he kept. I imagine he was mulling it over. She writes of her deepest sympathy but then refers to, what for her seemed to be, unresolved problems with Clyde. She praises Clyde, but says that before his untimely death, she had been thinking of moving out of the house *'in order no longer to be a source of trial to him'*. She had already begun to build her own cottage. Now she had no specific plans because she saw Marly needed her support. Apart from the fact that the letter is inappropriately long, there is something about it that I do not like; the barbed comments that I remember she sometimes made. I am sure he felt the same, and really did not know how to respond to, what on the face of it was, a very sympathetic letter. Perhaps there was a response, which was never kept.

Although he did not show it, my grandfather was devastated by Clyde's death. It subsequently proved to be the end of his marriage. Except for a couple of times on leave, which my grandmother mentioned in her letters, he hardly ever went home again. It was probably too painful. He had come to know Chute through Clyde's letters. It is evident from their correspondence that a true friendship was developing, probably the first my grandfather had ever had in his life, apart from his closeness to his sister Enid. Few of his letters remain and, apart from those to Clyde, they were all very formal. There were several books written about the battles and negotiations in which he took part. His work was applauded and people obviously admired and liked him but it seemed that already quite a private man, he retreated further. He had extremely good organizational skills, 'no fuss and bother', but there was no getting close to him. I remember him as a somewhat remote figure, kind and polite but rather aloof. Not that he was haughty, he obviously tried to be friendly, but somehow he was untouchable and unknowable. Like many of his generation, men were gentlemen and kept their feelings to themselves, and the course his life took from now on seemed to be extremely lonely. He had never been prepared for married life; like many products of an English public school system he had been trained not to show emotion. There were stories that he had a girlfriend somewhere, he was certainly debonair and handsome; my mother told me he had wanted to marry again, but I could find no evidence – possibly he was very discreet. When he retired he asked my grandmother to give him a divorce but she refused. She did not want what was then considered the 'shame' attached to being a divorcee, and anyway she liked being 'Lady' Morse, a title she gained from his knighthood at the end of the War. In deference to my grandmother he honourably dropped the matter.

On the 3rd February *Neptune* and *Force K* were in Freetown again when the damaged Exeter came in to be made sufficiently seaworthy to be taken back to England. The crew cleared the deck to cheer *Exeter*. It must have hit home again to my grandfather that Clyde, although a hero, was not there. He stayed on for a while in South Africa surveying the Atlantic shipping, burying his grief in his work and the fight against the Germans. The recent memories of Clyde and their time together in some ways must have been comforting, but also poignant. But there was a war to fight; and he had a true sense of duty and determination to make Clyde's death part of an overall victory for the Allies.

Chapter 20

England and the Blitz

1940-41

'We shall not flag or fail.'
Winston Churchill

Back at Chute, my grandmother was still coming to terms with Clyde's death. The War was coming closer to home. It was no longer a battle in a faraway place. Eventually she realized she must pull herself together. I can only imagine her grief at losing her only son so young, by putting myself in her place. In May the primroses appeared, very late after the long hard winter, and as the spring sun came, she must have decided she could no longer wallow in the sad reminders of all the things she and Clyde had planned together. Amongst the letters she had lovingly kept from South Africa, describing the walks they had taken, there was even one with detailed instructions and diagrams as to how she should use his gun while he was away, to keep down the rabbit population. She put it all behind her, and started to play her part in supporting those who were fighting so bravely. She organized a Primrose Party at Chute Collis with the local Women's Institute, and invited the members to come and pick the lovely, delicate smelling, pale yellow flowers that were in abundance in the surrounding woods. They gave them to six hospitals.

I notice Nan still wore a black armband for Clyde. She had joined the local Red Cross and trained as a nurse in Andover, and Mary volunteered to drive a truck for the Army base not far away up on the Wiltshire Downs, so they were both often out.

By the 14th June, German tanks had occupied Paris, and by the 16th the Rhone Valley. Northern, South-western France and its Atlantic coast were under German control. The French capitulated to German authority, seeing it as the only way to save France from annihilation, many feeling defeated and betrayed by the British after the exodus of Dunkirk. Marechal Petain, an 84-year-old First World War hero, signed an armistice with Germany and a new collaborative French State was established in the spa town of Vichy, using the empty hotels as their headquarters. They were hence known as the 'Vichy French' and nominally controlled the unoccupied zone of central and the South-eastern France. General Charles de Gaulle fled to London and from there, with the support of Churchill, broadcast instructions to his 'Free

French' movement by means of the BBC, organizing the Resistance and rallying support in the French colonies in Africa. So far the War was not going well for Britain; with France now occupied by the Germans, she was vulnerable to invasion.

The reality of the War was coming home to them now, and like the rest of the population they feared the threat of an invasion and England's safety. On June 4th 1940 Churchill gave another of his famous speeches in the House of Commons, which they listened to on the radio:

> "Turning once again, and this time more generally, to the question of invasion, I would observe that there has never been a period in all these long centuries of which we boast, when an absolute guarantee against invasion, still less against serious raids, could have been given to our people. In the days of Napoleon... the same wind which would have carried his transports across the Channel might have driven away the blockading fleet...We are assured that novel methods will be adopted, and when we see the originality of malice, the ingenuity of aggression, which our enemy displays, we may certainly prepare ourselves for every kind of novel stratagem and every kind of brutal and treacherous manœuvre. I think that no idea is so outlandish that it should not be considered and viewed with a searching, but I hope, steady eye. We must never forget the solid assurances of sea power...and air power, if it can be locally exercised. I have, myself, full confidence that if all do their duty, if nothing is neglected, and if the best arrangements are made, as they are being made, we shall prove ourselves once more able to defend our island home, to ride out the storm of war, and to outlive the menace of tyranny, if necessary for years, if necessary alone. At any rate, that is what we are going to try to do. That is the resolve of His Majesty's Government — every man of them. That is the will of Parliament and the nation. The British Empire and the French Republic, linked together in their cause and in their need, will defend to the death their native soil, aiding each other like good comrades to the utmost of their strength. Even though large tracts of Europe and many old and famous States have fallen or may fall into the grip of the Gestapo and all the odious apparatus of Nazi rule, **we shall not flag or fail.** We shall go on to the end. We shall fight in France, we shall fight on the seas and

oceans, we shall fight with growing confidence and growing strength in the air, we shall defend our island, whatever the cost may be. **We shall fight on the beaches, we shall fight on the landing grounds, we shall fight in the fields and in the streets, we shall fight in the hills; we shall never surrender,** and if, which I do not for a moment believe, this island or a large part of it were subjugated and starving, then our Empire beyond the seas, armed and guarded by the British Fleet, would carry on the struggle, until, in God's good time, the new world, with all its power and might, steps forth to the rescue and the liberation of the old."

Reading the speech again I understand why people rallied to Churchill's call, it is an admirable piece of rhetoric, sadly lacking in most politicians today.

In July my grandfather, like all those serving in the Forces, received a missive from Churchill. It set the general tone of how they were to command the fighting services, and gives a feeling of the mood at the time. He was by now in the Mediterranean, and so not directly affected by this part of the action, but the principle was the same wherever you were. My grandmother and mother, Jane, in England must have been in his thoughts.

4th July 1940
Letter to Captain J.A.V. Morse,D.S.O.
R.N.H.M.S PYRAMUS.
From:10, Downing Street,Whitehall.

On what may be the eve of an attempted invasion or battle for our native land, the Prime Minister desires to impress upon all persons holding responsible positions in the Government, in the Fighting Services, or in the Civil Department, their duty to maintain a spirit of alert and confident energy. While every precaution must be taken that time and means afford, there are no grounds for supposing that more German troops can be landed in this country, either from the air or across the sea, than can be destroyed or captured by the strong forces at present under arms. The Royal Air Force is in excellent order and at the highest strength it has yet attained. The German Navy was never so weak, nor the British Army at home so strong as now. The Prime Minister expects all His Majesty's servants in high places to set an example of steadiness and resolution. They should check and rebuke expressions of loose and ill-digested opinion in their circles, or by their subordinates. They should not hesitate to report, or if necessary remove, any officers or officials who are found to be consciously exercising a disturbing or depressing influence, and whose talk is calculated to spread alarm and despondency. Thus alone will they be worthy of the fighting men, who in the air, on the sea, and on land, have already met the enemy without any sense of being out-matched in martial qualities.

Winston S Churchill

At this point in the war the hospitals were becoming very full of wounded soldiers and there was a need for beds for convalescents. Like many people with big houses, my grandmother decided to offer Chute Collis as a place for soldiers to recuperate. At least they could be of some help to the War effort, and it stopped them feeling as if they were rattling around in a huge useless house. After Dunkirk they received some young soldiers to recuperate after fighting in France; they were followed by Australians, New Zealanders and South Africans, who all enjoyed their time there and became good friends, exercised the neglected ponies, and generally made themselves useful about the place. Mary even mowed and rolled the tennis lawn for them to play tennis, and she prepared the croquet lawn for those who were only able to take a gentler form of exercise.

My mother, Jane, more in touch with the younger generation, encouraged them to increase the vegetable garden in the "Dig For Victory" campaign. The Slade School of Art had been evacuated to Oxford where she had a cottage, and she was becoming involved in the 'Land Girl Army'. What she learnt became an important part of her life, and a balance to the heady and, in many ways nihilistic, life she was leading in Oxford. It held her in good stead years later, when bohemian life in London no longer had the same allure, and she wanted something healthier for us, her growing children. When I was eleven and my brother eight, my mother, with no previous experience but characteristic bravery, decided to leave it all behind, buy a smallholding in Dorset and take up farming. She loved and excelled at rural life.

"Dig for Victory" was the brainchild of the recently appointed Minister of Food, Lord Woolton. He was a charismatic man with sharp business acumen, who instigated and 'sold' the benefits of food rationing to the public. It meant every individual having a 'Ration Book' and registering at a local supplier, who took off the coupons as the goods were bought. I remember that until 1954, when I was nine, this continued in some form; meat was scarce and sweets were still rationed. I was not conscious then of the actual amounts, and out curiosity I looked up to see what the rations were during the War.

WW2 Food Rations

This is the ration for one adult per week.

BACON and HAM 4ozs (100g)

MEAT .... to the value of 1s.2d Sausages were not rationed but difficult to obtain: offal was originally unrationed but sometimes formed part of the meat ration

BUTTER 2ozs (50g)

CHEESE ...... 2ozs (50g) sometimes it rose to 4ozs (100g) and even up to 8ozs (225g)

MARGARINE 4ozs (100g)

COOKING FAT ...... 4ozs (100g) often dropping to 2ozs (50g)

MILK ...... 3 pints (1800ml) sometimes dropping to 2 pints (1200ml). Household (skimmed, dried) milk was available. This was 1 packet each 4 weeks

SUGAR 8ozs (225g)

PRESERVES ....1lb (450g) every 2 months

TEA 2ozs (50g)

EGGS ....1 shell egg a week if available, but at times dropping to 1 every two weeks

Dried eggs................1 packet each 4 weeks

SWEETS .... 12 ozs (350g) each 4 weeks

In addition, there was a monthly points system. For example, with the 16 points that you were allocated, you were allowed to buy one can of fish or meat, or 2lb (900g) of dried fruit, or 8lb (3.6kg) of split peas.

Babies and younger children, expectant and nursing mothers had concentrated orange juice and cod liver oil from Welfare Clinics, together with priority milk. This milk was also available to invalids. School meals were started in the war because mothers were working extremely long hours to help the war effort. Also people who worked were often given food in the work canteens, which supplemented the rations.

People managed with remarkably little when one thinks of the excess of food we now have. I remember the concentrated orange juice diluted in water – how good it had tasted when there were no oranges – I can almost taste it now; and the cod liver oil we had to take every morning – how disgusting it was, but we washed it down with the orange juice. When I went to my first school in London we were supplied with a third-of-a-pint bottle of milk for 'elevenses'. It had a silver foil cap we collected for 'the blind' or some other recycling, only then it was never called 'recycling'. Clothes were also rationed and often hand-me-downs.

When Lord Woolton realized that rationing alone would not feed people, he launched the idea of 'Dig for Victory', with the aid of a high profile advertising campaign. It was brilliantly designed, encouraging people to help the war-effort by growing their own food at home. Before the World War II Britain imported 55 million tons of food a year, largely from America and Canada by sea. The merchant shipping convoys carrying it were being attacked, sunk, and their cargos often stolen; Clyde and his companions had indeed died trying to keep these shipping lines clear. As the War escalated there was a need to fill the space, previously used for food, with essential materials for fighting. Woolton's campaign was hugely successful in educating people into better eating habits and economy, during and after the War; so much so that the wartime generation were in many ways one of the healthiest ever in Britain, and certainly much healthier than now. At the beginning of the 21st century, we are again in a supposed time of austerity, due to over-dependence on credit, and yet there is so much waste. On one side, there is obesity, heart problems and high cholesterol, and on the other, starvation. My mother, like most people who had lived through the War, never wasted anything and was very clever at using leftovers and making them appetizing. The campaign not only encouraged people all over Britain to transform their diets, but also to turn their private gardens, sports pitches and public parks into vegetable gardens and allotments; to grow food, keep chickens, rabbits and pigs, and to recycle scraps for animal food and compost. Not only were there posters, leaflets, booklets and radio programmes, but also hands-on demonstrations, organized to educate and show the public how to do it. This happened not only in the countryside but also in cities. In London the parks put aside flowerbeds to grow vegetables; Kew Gardens took part, and Hyde Park had a piggery.

At Chute, my grandmother kept chickens and they had plenty of wild rabbits. The vegetable garden had already provided most of their basic vegetables since they had moved in, but had been wiped out by the long hard winter. This year they had to do most of the work since Yorke, the gardener-cum-chauffer, had 'joined up'. Mary volunteered to do the digging, the chalky loamy soil of Chute was not heavy to dig, but composting was important and so they kept all the peelings. As soon as the ground was ready Marly drove the Baby Austin to nearby Andover to buy seeds.

Everyone in London, and other big cities, was preparing for a German invasion. On August 10th 1940 the Battle of Britain, or the Blitz, began. London and the whole of England, in particular airfields and cities where the Germans knew RAF airplanes were being produced, were subject to constant bombing attacks by the Luftwaffe. My grandmother thought they were relatively safe at Chute, but on Aug 14th the local airfield at Middle Wallop was bombed. Seven bombs fell near them in the middle of the night, shrapnel ripping the window curtains and whistling through the house. The housemaid, Phyllis, ran in her nightgown to see if anyone was hurt. They were fine, apart from being shaken, and the fact that the shrapnel had cut the electricity cable, so they were without power. Eventually they unearthed their camping primus stove and, in truly British style, made tea. Early the next morning my grandmother said she was rather annoyed. While she was trying to make up the lost sleep, she was awakened by sounds of yelling sightseers, locals on bicycles and ponies, even donkey carts, and some in cars (using their precious petrol allowances) coming to see what had happened. She was amazed at their ghoulish curiosity. She commented:

> *"At this early stage of the war bombs were a thrilling novelty in the wilds of Wiltshire, although Anthony on leave was later to say it was far more restful at sea, away from all the bombing. Later, while breakfasting, we had a visit from the local Air Warden who was much aggrieved, and angry with us, because the police knew of the bombing before he had been informed! We thought at first he had come to congratulate us on our wonderful escape! Following his visit came a neighbour, bringing a completely cooked luncheon of grouse and all the exceteras. 'I thought you would not be able to cook with no electricity' she said".*

On 7th September 1,000 Luftflotte set out for London in a daylight attack on the East End of London bombing it to bits. From 9th September for 57 consistent nights London was bombed every night until the following May 1941, when mercifully for the British, Hitler decided to concentrate his efforts on Russia and to left England in peace for a while.

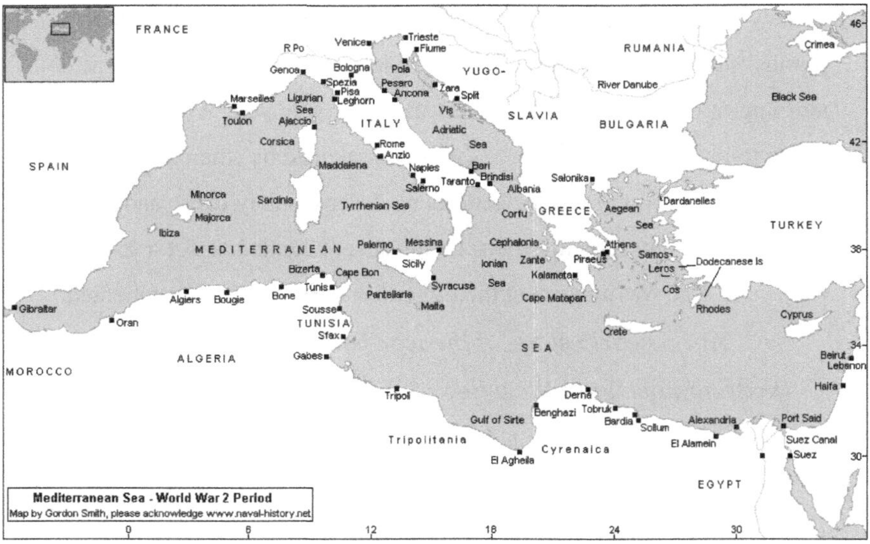

Mediterranean Sea - World War 2 Period
Map by Gordon Smith, please acknowledge www.naval-history.net

Chapter 21

"Mare Nostrum"

Mussolini and the Mediterranean

In April 1940 my grandfather took *Neptune* up to the Mediterranean and was transferred to Malta as part of the 7th Cruiser Squadron. He was serving under Admiral Cunningham (ABC), whom he had come to know and respect between the Wars; a gifted and courageous leader. My grandfather was probably relieved to be back in the Mediterranean and to start fighting seriously. Kind as people were, he must have found it difficult to go through all the various social functions he had to attend. Some of the invitations he kept, were evidence of this.

Villa Thilmere
Malta *April 27th 1940*

Dear Capt Morse,

Welcome to Malta! Conditions permitting - we should be very pleased if you could dine with us here on Thursday May 2nd at seven **(No)** *and go on to the Opera House with us to the Charity Concert in aid of Naval Comforts.*

We are also having a small captain's party on Thursday April 30th **(also No)** *and would love to have your company if you can manage it. We were very sorry to hear of your son's death in the River Plate Action please accept our deep sympathy.*

We look forward to seeing 'ere you depart in every direction!

Yours sincerely, Eve

In his neat spidery writing he had scribbled 'No' refusing this one, but probably there were others he had to attend.

He had plenty to occupy him. The British controlled the Mediterranean. Malta was Britain's most important Mediterranean naval base and was destined to play a frontline role. It was in a good position to protect east-west supply lines, and block the passage between Italy and her North African Empire in Libya. Oil was vital for the weaponry of this war, and the Middle East and North Africa were where it came from.

In May, one of his midshipmen recorded in his diary:

> "May 27th 1940 Captain Morse addressed ship's company saying 'he was very sorry that he had not taken us into action and brought us home victorious'. He was relieved by Captain O'Conor."

From now on his tasks were to be different. He was to be based along with the French, Australians and New Zealanders in Alexandria, 'awaiting developments' and 'sweeping the Med'. Apart from Malta, the British had bases in Gibraltar, Cyprus, Alexandria and the Suez Canal. My grandfather operated in the Eastern Mediterranean, spending the next couple of years transporting troops and arranging evacuations. Reading the accounts of the battles and my grandfather's part in them, I realized that war is as much to do with the preparations – the everyday care of troops, food supplies, entertainment and discipline – as with the battle and evacuations. Much of the success or failure of a campaign is to do with the communications between the various officers in charge and their troops. My grandfather, now fifty, was given commands of this nature, less daring than in the First War, but he had a gift for creating order out of chaos, and in very unfavourable circumstances he acquitted himself honourably and well.

Nazi Germany's involvement in the Mediterranean was due to Mussolini. Hitler was not really interested in the Mediterranean; he had his eyes on Russia. Mussolini did not much care for Hitler, and did not want to play second fiddle to him. By entering the War on June 10th 1940 on the German side, he hoped to realize his dream to re-establish the Roman Empire and control of the Mediterranean. He had a strong Navy *(Regia Marina)* and in true Italian style the ships were beautifully designed; they were as light and fast manoeuvring as the German ones were heavy and unwieldy. On June 11th Italian Stuka aircraft attacked the dockyards of Malta. The Maltese were not ready. They had only forty-two anti-aircraft guns, two-dozen searchlights, and three small Gloster Gladiator biplanes that they discovered in crates and hurriedly assembled. The Gladiators they christened Faith, Hope and Charity. Although it seemed hopeless to fight off two hundred Stukas based 100km north in Sicily, by keeping up continuous firing and forcing the enemy to bomb from a greater height, they managed to hold their own. For three long weeks they bravely defended Malta's airspace. Only in August were they relieved by the arrival of twelve Hurricanes brought out from England.

Britain's interests in North Africa and the Middle East were in danger. In Libya, Eritrea and Abyssinia, Commander-in-chief of the Middle East, General Sir Archibald Wavell was facing vastly superior numbers – half a million Italian and Italian-colonial troops. He had only 50,000 troops, mostly in Sudan, Kenya and Egypt, and Churchill was reluctant to send him reinforcements because of the situation on the Home Front after Dunkirk. Wavell, however, took advantage of the lack of organization of the Italian troops, and managed to use his small armoured division to continuously harass the Italian posts on the frontier, penetrating right into the desert. Lieutenant-General Richard O'Connor and his 'Desert Rats', as they were later called, became the scourge of the Italian army. From June to September they lost only 150 men, compared to the Italians' loss of 3,500 men, and 130,000 who were taken prisoner; the British destroyed nearly 500 tanks and more than 1,000 guns. In August, while England was being heavily bombed every night during the 'The Blitz', Mussolini decided to seize the moment and attack western Egypt and Sudan. By mid-September, Churchill finally dispatched three more armoured regiments in three fast merchant ships via Gibraltar.

In October 1940, frustrated by his lack of success in Africa and Hitler's lack of interest in his opinions on war policy, Mussolini invaded Greece. Hitler was infuriated because he had wanted Greece to remain neutral and he did not want the British interfering in the Balkans. The Greek forces bravely defended their territory, driving the Italians back and occupying part of Albania. Four days later, Hitler ordered his staff to prepare an invasion of Greece via Bulgaria and Romania. Mussolini had left him with no alternative. The Greeks knew they could not stand up to the Germans. King George II of Greece appealed to his cousin, George VI, for help. Churchill responded by putting pressure on Admiral Cunningham to clear up the situation in the

Mediterranean. He was desperate for a breakthrough somewhere – Malta was still under heavy bombardment, there was little success in North Africa, and they were being bombed at home.

In early November there was a breakthrough. Admiral Cunningham managed, in one night, to halve the Italian fleet lying in the Bay of Taranto, losing only two small planes. There was no resistance from the air – it happened to be the day Mussolini had volunteered his Air Force to take part in the Blitz attacks on London. As a result of Taranto, the Italians withdrew the bulk of their fleet further north to Naples, thereby leaving Crete much freer as an alternative to Malta. On 4th November the British seized the opportunity to occupy Crete and get there before the Germans and Italians.

In December 1940, the German air force (*Fliegerkorps* X) moved into Sicily, to support the Italians and "wipe Malta off the map". Two hundred and fifty aircraft, together with German and Italian submarines, maintained a relentless assault on the supply convoys. The 10th January marked the beginning of a continuous effort to sink *HMS Illustrious* and destroy Malta's densely populated docks. Civilian casualties were very high. The situation in Greece was still unresolved. At the beginning of January 1941, the Greek Prime Minister General Metaxas, again appealed to Churchill for help. Although he was a fascist and like many Greeks admired the Germans, he preferred to side with Britain, and he was encouraged by his anglophile king.

Meanwhile in Libya, on 22nd January 1941, Wavell and O'Connor were having more success. They made another swift attack and drove the Italian Army as far back as Tobruk, almost destroying the whole Italian army in North Africa. Finally there was some news of success. The victory was hailed with much publicity and jubilation in England, as Tobruk was one of the few good harbours between Alexandria and Tripoli.

Churchill, however, felt he could not abandon the Greeks and was concerned about the situation in the Balkans. He offered a small contingent of the troops, which had been destined for Tobruk, to General Metaxas who refused, saying that the force was too small to guarantee an outright victory. By the end of the month, however, General Metaxas had died and the new Prime Minister accepted Churchill's offer.

In February, Wavell had to halt his advance into Libya – his best-trained troops had been ordered to Greece. He protested, but in the end the good soldier followed orders and reluctantly left the recently captured Tobruk under siege, in the hands of a small Australian division who had insufficient training. The move was a disaster and led to the loss of Tobruk, and an excuse for Churchill's virtual dismissal of Wavell.

On March 1st the Germans crossed the Danube, invaded Bulgaria and were clearly on their way to Greece. On March 7th 1941, 50,000 British Empire troops, General Wilson's *Force W,* landed in Greece from Alexandria. After months fighting in the Libyan desert, the troops recorded that they were pleased to be welcomed to a land of olive groves and spring flowers, surrounded by blue sea. The people welcomed them enthusiastically.

At sea, in all the difficulties and quarrels about where thinly stretched troops should go in the Mediterranean area, Admiral Cunningham on *HMS Warspite* came to the rescue, in another stunning victory against the Italian Navy at Matapan. There was a lot of activity from German reconnaissance planes to the south and west of Greece and Crete, as far as Alexandria. Cunningham, using the new breakthrough in Ultra intercepts that the British were making with Enigma at Bletchley Park, calculated that the Italian Fleet, of 13 ships and 17 destroyers, was about to leave Taranto Bay. Obviously they would not, if they knew he was waiting with 3 battleships and an aircraft carrier. So he devised a clever plan to outwit them.

On 27th March, ABC took *Warspite* and his fleet back to Alexandria, so that the Italians would think they were refuelling. He directed his Vice-Admiral Henry Pridham-Wippell, with 4 light cruisers and 4 destroyers, to sail south from Greece and lure the Italians south towards him, if he encountered them first. He then went to his club in Alexandria, where he knew the Japanese Consul was playing golf. He was a large fellow (nicknamed 'the blunt end of the Axis' on account of his broad behind, particularly noticeable when he was putting a stroke!), and was well known for reporting shipping movements to the Germans and Italians. Cunningham played a round of golf with him, making much of having a large overnight suitcase with him. Once it was dark, he returned to *Warspite* and the fleet sailed at 7pm. At 06:50 on 28th March, the Italian planes spotted Pridham-Wippell's ships and turned to race towards them, but their poor gunnery failed to score any major hits. Pridham-Wippell's fleet managed to escape. ABC on *Warspite* arrived with his fleet and *Formidable,* with six Fairey Albacore torpedo bombers, attacked and badly damaged *Vittorio Veneto,* slowing her down considerably. Once dark had fallen, ABC, who was highly skilled at night fighting, using radar, surprised *Zara* and *Fiume*. In less than ten minutes he had destroyed them. He then took possession of the crippled *Pola*, removed her crew and had her scuppered. The Battle of Cape Matapan was a decisive victory for the Royal Navy and gave it control of the eastern Mediterranean until the fall of Crete in June. The British lost only three men (the crew of one torpedo bomber), while the Italians lost 3 heavy cruisers, 2 destroyers, with over 2,400 dead. After the battle Cunningham continued his pursuit of the Italians but was forced to turn back when German bombers appeared overhead. In his usual compassionate way, he radioed Rome, letting the Italian headquarters know the location of the battle's survivors, and then left the area. The battle was disaster for the *Regia Marina* and effectively broke its back; the next time it emerged in force was to surrender to Cunningham in 1943. A few weeks after the battle Cunningham went to personally thank the women at Bletchley for their contribution to the victory.

On April 2nd Hitler sent Rommel to reinforce the Italians in North Africa. Leading the *Africa Corps,* he forced the British to retreat back from Benghazi. A group of Australians, with extreme courage and bravery, managed to hold out at Tobruk, from April 11th 1941 for 240 days; they were backed up by the Navy who provided gunfire support, supplies, fresh troops and ferried out the wounded.

Early in the morning of April 6th 1941, the Germans invaded Greece. General Metaxas was proved right. General Wilson's *Force W,* along with the Greek troops, was no match for the Germans and Italians. They could not hold them. They tried to defend some of the passes, even the narrow Thermopylae, but German armour was superior in number, and quality. The troops found themselves in the snow-covered Greek Highlands, fighting and sleeping in the perishing cold of craggy mountains and yawning ravines. They were hopelessly ill equipped. Many of the Australians were using donkeys for hauling ammunition and food supplies, both of which were in short supply. The German Messerschmitts flew overhead day and night, shooting everything in sight. Luckily, there was quite a bit of cover in the caves in the mountains. The Luftwaffe destroyed Athens, and attacked the port of Piraeus where more troops were disembarking. The Allies started a race south through Greece, but on 17th April the defeated Greek Prime Minister shot himself, and King George II had to take over. On the 23rd the King and the government fled to Crete, and by the 24th General Wilson had to arrange for a swift evacuation. The weary troops made their way to the beaches to be picked up by the Royal Navy, who welcomed them with big mugs of cocoa, fresh bread and a slab of beef with mustard. 'Safe in the hands of the Navy' they sailed for Crete. Much of their material had to be destroyed or left behind, including at least 8,000 almost new vehicles, most artillery and heavy equipment recently transported from Alexandria, including even radio sets, rifles and mortars. Nearly 300 New Zealanders had been killed in the few weeks of fighting, and 1,800 captured. It seemed like a repeat of 'Dunkirk'. There were 15,000 casualties in all and by 27th April Greece was in the hands of the Germans. Over 50,000 Allied troops were evacuated to Crete by the end of the month.

Map by Gordon Smith,
www.naval-history.net

Chapter 22

The Battle for Suda Bay

April 1941

Once he had Greece, Hitler turned his attention to Crete. The island would give him a good base in the Mediterranean, and prevent the British using it to mount bombing raids against the Romanian oilfields, and getting into the Balkans. It would not disrupt his plans in Europe.

The British Navy, once the troops from Greece had been rescued, also turned its attention to the defence of Crete. Two contingents of Marines were brought from Alexandria under Major-General Weston. The New Zealand and Australian troops arriving from Greece straggled into the north of the island, some to Suda Bay, others to Maleme and Canea. At first there was little organization, many found themselves an olive grove and recuperated by sleeping, playing cards and foraging what rations they could from the locals. They were pretty desperate for a good meal and a bed to sleep in; they had had a rough time in Greece. Some, with time on their hands, sampled the local red wine and there were a few incidents of bad behaviour.

My grandfather as, Captain Morse, Naval Officer-in-Charge at Suda Bay Harbour, arrived accompanied by his deputy Commander C Wauchope, on April 22nd 1941. They tried to put some order into things between the various commands. His initial report was:

"The effect of the evacuation of Greece on Crete was a great increase in the number to be fed and maintained without any great increase in fighting force. Such fighting troops as became available were poorly equipped and had suffered severely in Greece. Their morale was not high and the conditions under which they were forced to live did not improve matters..."

A force of 30,000 British troops, 11,000 Greeks and 15,000 Italian prisoners, amongst a population of 400,000, even in peacetime, could not be fed from the island's resources. Somehow all these people had to be supplied. On May 14th six tanks arrived – they were to be the sum of the Allies armoured defence throughout the whole battle. German and Italian aircraft kept up a steady attack on the troops and ships as they docked with supplies. In his reports Captain Morse said:

"as the scale of air attack increased, the supply of labour decreased! Cypriot labour had proved completely unsatisfactory."

He had to use Australian and New Zealand soldiers to unload the ships. They had now recovered in the spring sunshine, with frequent swims in the blue waters of the Aegean. They: *"gave excellent service under the most trying conditions*", but had to unload at night. Between 29th April and 20th May, they managed to run in 15 ships, 8 of which were sunk or damaged by air attacks, and offload 15,000 tons of supplies and men, which had to be got ashore and convoyed to different parts of the island.

On 30th April General Wavell arrived and asked Major General Bernard Freyberg, Commander of the Second New Zealand Expeditionary Force, to take charge of 'Creforce'. He was a brave and well-loved Australian leader, who had survived the previous war with honour. Freyberg assessed the situation and realized that it was chaotic. The troops were poorly equipped and there were not even picks and shovels to build latrines. The Luftwaffe, now redeployed to Greek airfields, bombed Suda Bay Harbour daily, while they were trying to build up adequate defences and ship in reinforcements. Anchorage was limited, so they had to use Alexandria as the base of operations – 420 miles away.

They expected the German invasion on 17th May. The plan was that Admiral Cunningham should cover the most likely landing places to the north of the island – Canea, Retimo, Heraklion, Kisamos Bay and Sitia, and carry out sweeps at night. They knew Hitler did not have a Navy to match up to the British, and expected the attack by sea, so they thought they were well prepared. Part of the fleet would be kept in port against the possibility of fuel shortages, and there would be some air reconnaissance, although meagre. What they did not anticipate was the force of the German attack from the air, which a young German paratroop specialist, General Kurt Student, had suggested to Hitler. On 19th the skies rained parachutes and gliders onto Crete's three airfields. Aided by Cretan civilians, the 7,500 New Zealand, British, Australian and Greek troops, almost succeeded in fighting off this huge airborne attack. The soldiers had only their personal weapons, ammunition and

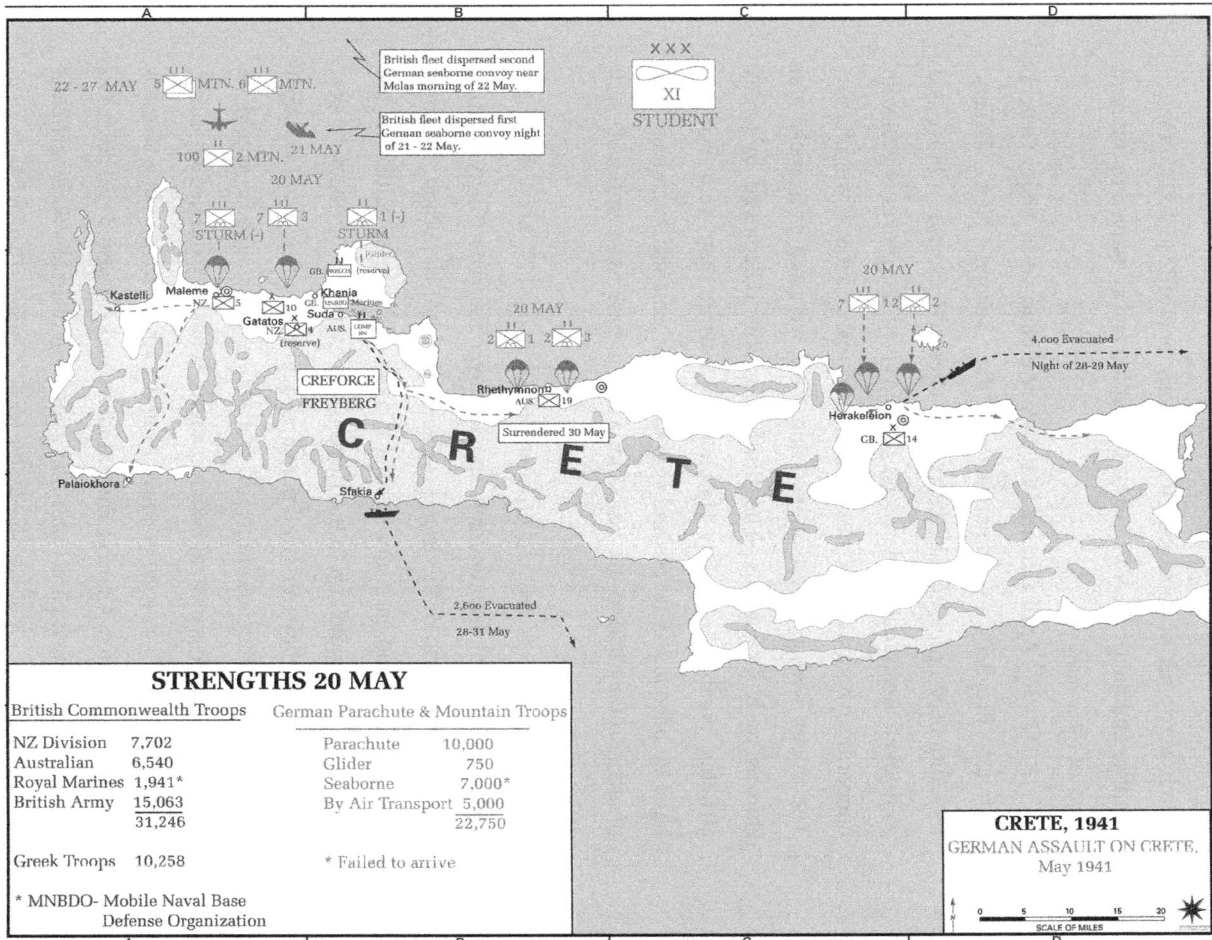

CRETE, 1941
GERMAN ASSAULT ON CRETE, May 1941
British fleet dispersed second German seaborne convoy near Melas morning of 22 May.
British fleet dispersed first German seaborne convoy night of 21 - 22 May.
XXX
XI
STUDENT
22 - 27 MAY
5 MTN.
6 MTN.
100
2 MTN.
21 MAY
20 MAY
7 STURM (-)
7 3
1 (-) STURM
GB.
(reserve)
Kastelli
Maleme
NZ. 5
10
Khania
Suda
Gatatos
NZ. 4
(reserve)
AUS.
Marines
CREFORCE
FREYBERG
Palaiokhora
Sfakia
20 MAY
2 1
2 3
Rhethymnon
AUS. 19
Surrendered 30 May
20 MAY
7 1 2 2
Herakeleion
GB. 14
4,000 Evacuated
Night of 28-29 May
2,600 Evacuated
28-31 May
C R E T E
STRENGTHS 20 MAY
British Commonwealth Troops
NZ Division 7,702
Australian 6,540
Royal Marines 1,941*
British Army 15,063
31,246
Greek Troops 10,258
* MNBDO- Mobile Naval Base Defense Organization
German Parachute & Mountain Troops
Parachute 10,000
Glider 750
Seaborne 7,000*
By Air Transport 5,000
22,750
* Failed to arrive
0 5 10 15 20
SCALE OF MILES

guns were in short supply. Nevertheless, they shot many of the parachutists down before they could land and stand up, and in this way usually gained another weapon. Big weapons – tanks and guns – were few and far between.

On the morning of 20th from his headquarters in Suda Bay, my grandfather could see the attack on Maleme and Canea, and then that afternoon, the Luftwaffe flew over Suda Bay bombing and machine gunning the harbour and ships.

In the middle of all this, Col J. Blunt, the British Military Attaché to the Greek Government, managed to take the King of Greece from Canea where he was staying, south over the hills into hiding. They spent the night in the small, almost deserted village of Panashia. The next day Blunt miraculously spotted a telephone booth with a functioning telephone. He rang the Royal Naval Command in Suda Bay, who was my grandfather. Blunt left a brief message with the telephone operator, not referring to the King by name, saying they needed a prearranged evacuation in forty-eight hours. My grandfather sent one back saying: "I completely understand the message and will now make all arrangements for the night of Thursday May 22nd." Footsore and weary they arrived at the rendezvous at Ayia Roumeli to a rather surreal, but probably welcome, scene. Lady Palairet, the British Ambassador's wife, had set three tables in horse-shoe pattern under the trees, and decorated them with vine leaves, asphodel and anemones. The King and his Cabinet members dined on milky soup, corned beef and boiled potatoes. Finally, they got the prearranged signal that the *HMS Decoy* was in the bay below awaiting them. Blunt later said: "The fortune of war was certainly with us, but on the march I spent a good deal of time with my fingers crossed. We got away from the farm without being spotted from the air. We collected mules and managed to avoid the German parachutists. No one broke a limb by falling on the steep mountain slopes, we reached the rendezvous dead on time and were picked up by the destroyer *Decoy*." They were evacuated to Alexandria, along with Greek and Cretan civilians, and some of the British and Greek forces.

On 23rd May, the situation on the island worsened dramatically. The troops were forced to withdraw from Maleme airfield. Enemy gliders were still landing continuously, almost unopposed. Some British soldiers tried to enlist the help of the Cretan gendarmerie as guerrillas, and drove down to Suda Bay the next morning in search of some arms and equipment, which were expected from Alexandria. Most of the parachutists by this time had been mopped up on the Akrotiri peninsular and the road was clear, but Suda Bay itself was not at all a healthy spot. The harbour was being bombed incessantly and was littered with half-submerged wrecks. One report said:

> "Amid this scene of desolation Captain J.A.V Morse, the senior naval officer, seemed the only person entirely unperturbed. He said that nothing had arrived from Alexandria, but that a mine-laying destroyer was due in late that night and that if it had anything, he would try to let them know."

For a day or two more the battle hung in the balance, but on the third day the Germans captured Maleme airfield, and then took the other airfields on the north shore. After four days, the troops were forced to retreat through the wild mountains to the southern shore. Most of them walked, they left their equipment on the way and arrived at the beaches exhausted and hungry, their boots in shreds. There were also hundreds of civilians to contend with, and all sorts of people with no formation, order or cohesion. Men struggled to board boats off open beaches, requisitioned or stole fishing boats.

My grandfather now reported:

"General situation in Suda-Canea area very bad and General Officer Commanding decided that he could no longer continue the battle. Preparations made for evacuation and movements of H.Q. and W/T to Sfakia. Confusion all day due to lack of definite orders. P.M. burnt all unwanted secret papers."

At 10 p.m. the following day, having destroyed the port wireless station, the remaining members of the base staff in a

"convoy of lorries and cars left G.H.Q. for Sfakia. Progress very slow on account of bad road and thousands of disorganized retreating troops."

He and Freyberg moved their headquarters to a cave near the small fishing village of Skafia. On the 26th May General Freyberg signaled General Wavell: "Limit of endurance has been reached by troops under my command here at Suda Bay."

Skafia had a shingle beach, only a short stretch of which could be used for embarking in boats. It was walled in by a 500-foot high escarpment and access was by goat track, which took at least two hours to climb down. My grandfather said:

"the difficulty was to get troops down to the beach quickly enough, communication between the beach and those on the escarpment hiding from air observation, had to be maintained on foot."

On the first night he signaled Cunningham:

"up to 1,000 will be ready to embark".

Two hundred and thirty men from each battalion of the 4th Brigade were selected, and the 28th Maori Battalion. Fifth Brigade stayed holding an inner perimeter around the village. Once down on the beach, there was a rough and dangerous passage to the troopship. The soldiers had to clamber on board, calling for speed and more speed, and there was a race to get clear of the coast before the inevitable arrival of the Luftwaffe. The sailors were in many cases as weary and hungry as the soldiers they were rescuing, and over everything there was the depressing feeling of defeat. The destroyers lifted a total of 7,449 troops and sailed at 3 a.m. on the 29th. On the passage to Alexandria, four aircraft bombed them for half and hour, and *Nizam* sustained minor damage from near misses. They reached Alexandria without further incident at 5 p.m. that day.

By May 30th the Battle of Crete was over. It was in the hands of the Germans. The evacuation was exactly one year after Dunkirk, but with none of the same glory. The Navy had fought well and managed to thwart any attempt by the German ships to get to Crete, but the British superiority at sea could not balance the German domination of the air. The British lost one out of every two of their soldiers in Crete. Both sides had fought bravely but with a tremendous cost. Both the British decision to defend Crete, and the German's to seize the island, in retrospect seemed ill-considered. Captain Morse and General Freyberg were some of the last to leave on the night of May 30/31. The evacuation had to be abandoned and some troops were left behind because the ships could no longer return. Some men managed to make it to Egypt on their own, others fought on as guerrillas.

As they were landing in Egypt, the men received the following message from General Wavell:

"I thank you for the great courage and endurance with which you attempted the defence of the Island of Crete. I am well aware of the difficulties under which you carried out your task and that it must have appeared to many of you that you had been asked to do the impossible, and that you were insufficiently equipped and supported. As

Commander-in-Chief, I accept responsibility for what was done. It was for strategic reasons necessary to hold the Island of Crete...You are aware of the courage and skill with which the Navy brought you back from Crete; I have on your behalf sent them a message of gratitude...."

It was tantamount to an apology.

Admiral Cunningham wrote in his dispatches, following the campaign:

> "More than once I felt that the stage had been reached when no more could be asked of officers and men, physically and mentally exhausted by their efforts and by the events of these fateful weeks. It is perhaps, even now, not realized how nearly the breaking point was reached, but that these men struggled through is the measure of their achievement, and I trust that it will not lightly be forgotten . . .The Mediterranean Fleet paid a heavy price for the achievement. Losses and damage were sustained which would normally only occur during a major fleet action, in which the enemy fleet might be expected to suffer greater losses than our own. In this case the enemy fleet did not appear (though it had many favourable opportunities for doing so) and the battle was fought between ships and aircraft."

As for my grandfather's part:

From London Gazette 21st May 1948

THE BATTLE OF CRETE

The following Despatch was submitted to the Lords Commissioners of the Admiralty on 4th August 1941, *by Admiral Sir Andrew B. Cunningham, G.C.B., D.S.O., Commander-in-Chief, Mediterranean.*

14. The Naval Officer-in-Charge, Suda, Captain J. A. V. Morse, D.S.O., Royal Navy, followed up his excellent work in organising the port at Suda by consistently presenting a clear and concise picture of the situation by his signals during the battle. His presence at Suda was invaluable. A B CUNNINGHAM

Chapter 23

Senior Naval Officer Levant 1941-2

The War trundled on with heavy losses of life on all fronts and increasing hardship at home in Britain. I found that there were a few photographs in my grandmother's album. There seemed to be no letters kept from my grandfather, if indeed he wrote any. He had a lot of demands on him, and I imagine it was quite difficult to communicate with home. Most of the information I had from now on was from Admiralty reports, and in books dealing with World War II in the Mediterranean. He now moved to Beirut where he played a vital part in negotiations.

Events in Greece immediately provoked a crisis in Iraq. British interests there were threatened by a coup in Baghdad by Rashid Ali al Gaylani, a violently anti-British Arab nationalist. He had the support of the exiled grand mufti of Jerusalem, Amin al-Husseini, a charismatic Islamic cleric, who was also fervently anti-British as a result of the Balfour Declaration in 1917, when Palestine was handed over to the Zionists. The Germans, Italians and Vichy French backed them. Supplies from the northern oilfields were in danger, and the air link and land route between India and Egypt was severed. This, in turn, subverted the tenuous position held by Britain in Egypt and Palestine.

In early May 1941, Churchill ordered Wavell to march from Palestine to Iraq across the desert, to relieve the besieged British air base at Habbaniya, and assume overall control of troops in Iraq. Wavell protested that his hands were already full, and even with enough forces, this was hardly the moment to ignite Arab volatility. He recommended a more diplomatic approach. But Churchill was adamant, and it fell to Auchinleck's India Command to send troops to Basra. Hope of a quick victory in Iraq, however, faded as the Vichy French put up a determined defence. Wavell, after evacuating Greece, somewhat reluctantly, sent General Wilson to assist. By end of May, Iraqforce had captured Baghdad and the Anglo-Iraqi War ended, with troops in Iraq once more reverting to the overall control of GHQ in Delhi.

The whole affair produced a stalemate between Wavell and Churchill, who had been unimpressed by Wavell's lack of enthusiasm over Greece and subsequently Iraq. Churchill was determined to relieve him of his command. In mid-June, after *Operation Battleaxe* had failed to relieve Tobruk, Churchill told Wavell that he was to be replaced by General Auchinleck, whose quick response had impressed him during the Iraq crisis. Wavell was sent to India as Commander-in-Chief, in an exchange of jobs with Auchinleck. It is interesting to note that in spite of Churchill's lack of confidence in him, Wavell was much admired by his peers. Auchinleck was impressed by the difficult job he had done, and even though he was not successful against his enemy Rommel in Libya, Rommel always rated Wavell highly, and carried a translation of his book '*Generals and Generalship'* in his pocket throughout his North Africa Campaign.

In the 1940's Beirut was a glamorous cosmopolitan city, often referred to as 'The Paris of the Middle East'. Since the dismantling of the Ottoman Empire and the Sykes Picot Agreement in 1916, it had been under French Mandate, which after the fall of France meant the Vichy French. The city looks out onto the sparkling blue Mediterranean and is backed by snow covered mountains and the famous cedars of Lebanon. Steeped in history – of Phoenicians, Crusaders and Ottomans – it is an important commercial centre. Its conflicts were always commercial and religious, with constant feuds between the Maronites. Alawites, Druzes, Sunnis and Shias.

On 8th July 1941, the Vichy French commander, General Henry Dentz, High Commissioner to the Levant States, lost control of the Northern Desert and the Euphrates Province and was in danger of losing Beirut. He sent Auchinleck a wireless message on the evening of the 11th July, proposing the end of hostilities six hours later at midnight, but only if they could exclude the Free French from the negotiations. The Middle East War Council considered his proposals, but the American Consul at Beirut decided that Dentz was playing for time; in the hope the Germans would rescue him. The British rejected his conditions and told him to send his representatives to the British outpost on the Beirut-Haifa Road, before nine the next morning. Dentz sent his second in command, Lieutenant-General Joseph-Antoine-Sylvain-Raoul de Verdillac, who, a later issue of Time Magazine suggested, was more pro-British and less anti-De Gaulle than himself. De Verdillac came from Syria to the outskirts of the city of Acre, in the British Mandate of Palestine, where the Armistice talks were held in the officer's mess of 'Sidney Smith Barracks'. They were the first between Britain and France since Napoleon's day. In spite of the generous terms offered by the British, the representatives of Vichy made a brief show of refusing them. Finally at 10 pm on 12th July 1941, the Armistice of Saint Jean d'Acre was initialled. On July 14th, General Dentz signed Syria and Lebanon away to the British and Free French Forces. The Allied forces were represented by General Wilson, Army; Air Commodore L. O Brown, Royal Air Force; my grandfather, Captain J. A. V. Morse, Royal Navy, General Georges Catroux for the Free French, and de Verdillac for the Vichy French. Ominously, when General de Verdillac uncapped his pen to add his signature, all the lights in the room suddenly fused. In order to complete the ceremony, a dispatch rider's motorbike was brought from outside to light the room with its headlamp. The Australian 7th Division recently arrived from Tobruk marched triumphantly into Beirut and successfully established the Allied occupation of Lebanon. This marked the end of hostilities in the Syria Lebanon campaign. The ceasefire came into effect at one minute past midnight. For all intents and purposes, this ended the campaign.

My grandfather is standing in the centre of a group with General Auchinleck on his left and General Henry Maitland Wilson on his right, after the signing of the Armistice of Saint Jean d'Acre ending the Syria-Lebanon Campaign.

Departure of Vichy French, General Crystal and my grandfather,.

My grandfather was appointed Senior Naval Officer Levant Area. He was stationed at Beirut, which from then on became an important Allied base for Mediterranean naval operations. He was in command of British and Free French Naval forces; and all British and Syrian ports in the area enclosed by a line from the Egypt-Palestine border to the Turkish coast. He was responsible for the control and escort of all merchant shipping in the Levant Area, excluding Palestinian ports.

Chapter 24

Pearl Harbour

'The bright gleam of victory'
Churchill

On December 7th 1941, while German armies were freezing before Moscow, something happened that was to change the course of the war – Pearl Harbour.

Since the 1930's, when my grandfather was in China, there had been a threat from the Japanese. They still bore a grudge against the Allies for their treatment at Versailles; they aligned themselves with the 'have-nots' in what amounted to a colonial carve up. In December 1941, exasperated with the Allies, most recently because of British and American oil and trade embargos, the Japanese attacked the American naval base at Pearl Harbour, Hawaii. They had carefully studied ABC's successful attack on the Italian Navy in Taranto Bay, and they used similar tactics. Roosevelt and the American nation were surprised and shocked; Japan struck before giving any official declaration of War. The Japanese had a well-trained, efficient Navy and strong Air Force, and were well prepared in terms of aircraft carriers. The attack was devastating. Even though the American cryptologists had broken the Japanese diplomatic code, the Navy in Pearl harbour were taken unawares. It is still disputed as to why, and whether Roosevelt and Churchill knew beforehand.

For Britain, it was almost in answer to Churchill's prayers, although he had the worry of South East Asia, which was now being invaded by the Japanese. They were concerned for Australia for a while. Singapore – considered by the British as the 'Gibraltar of the East' – was taken by the Japanese on February 15th 1942. This was followed by the occupation of Hong Kong, Burma, Thailand and Rangoon.

The attack on Pearl Harbour marked a turning point in the War for the Allies, as it ended the American Isolationism. Roosevelt had been secretly helping Britain by selling arms and lending money; but the American voters, until now, did not support the idea of their young men being killed in a War which seemed nothing to do with them. Four days after Pearl Harbour, Hitler declared war on the United States, and Roosevelt was able to persuade Congress to agree to immediate and massive expansion of the armed forces. Churchill went hurrying to America on a dangerous transatlantic journey aboard *HMS York,* and gave an historic speech on 26th December 1941, encouraging them to take part in the War. He then spent the Christmas holiday with Roosevelt and his wife, Eleanor, as their guest at the White House. On the first day of 1942, Churchill and Roosevelt, along with representatives of China and the Soviet Union, signed a declaration creating the United Nations, an alliance that eventually grew to include twenty-six countries and form the nucleus of a lasting international organization.

For the next year, Churchill worked on his special relationship with his most important ally. They often differed over questions of grand strategy; one source of division between Churchill and Roosevelt was the British Empire. The Prime Minister famously announced that he had "not become the King's First Minister to preside over the liquidation of the British Empire." Nonetheless, in an effort to keep America happy, and India loyal to Britain during the war, Churchill sent British statesman, Sir Stafford Cripps, to India with a plan for self-government in 1942. The mission failed when Gandhi's Congress Party would not agree. On the whole he had a good relationship with Roosevelt, and they were able to resolve many issues in the course of face-to-face meetings in Washington, and later, in January 1943, at a conference in Casablanca. Once the Americans were part of the fight there was a general feeling of optimism, that the Allies would eventually win the War. How long it would take, and how many more lives and battles it would cost, nobody knew.

In early 1942, British and American leaders reaffirmed the priority of winning back Europe. General Marshall argued for an immediate build up of American forces in England and they started arriving in January. Part of the plan was a possible diversionary attack on the Continent in the autumn, and a definite full-scale invasion in 1943. Churchill was cautious, remembering the enormous casualties in France in World War I, and then Dunkirk. Although he acknowledged the eventual necessity for an invasion of France, he hoped to defer it until later. He preferred to strike at German power in the Mediterranean, what he called '*the underbelly of the axis*', rather than risk a direct confrontation without careful planning. He suggested Anglo-American landings in Morocco, Algeria and Tunisia, which were nominally in the hands of the Vichy French. The idea was to bring the French armies in those colonies back into the War on the side of the Allies, thereby aiding the British in their fight against the Italians, and the German forces of Field Marshal Erwin Rommel. Months of lively debate followed, but ultimately President Roosevelt directed General Marshall to carry out amphibious landings on the coast of North Africa before the end of 1942.

The leader of the Free French, General Charles de Gaulle, although an ally, was a thorn in both their sides. In 1940, as France fell to the Nazis, Churchill recognized de Gaulle as 'the man of destiny', but their relationship turned into a roller coaster of mutual admiration, suspicion and, on Churchill's part, loathing. Roosevelt considered the French leader more trouble, and more infuriating, than any other person in the Second World War. Churchill, to his extreme embarrassment, found himself caught in the middle of an extraordinary arms-length duel between the President, who was the most powerful man in the world, and the French general, who put saving the honour of his devastated country above everything else. Nevertheless they had to work with him.

As an ally, Stalin was almost as troublesome. Their meetings did not always go smoothly. In August 1942, while the Russians were fighting for their lives before Stalingrad, Churchill flew to Moscow to tell him that there would be no Second Front in Western Europe to draw off German forces. Berating the British for their failure to come to grips with the Germans, Stalin said that British soldiers would lose their fear as soon as they started to fight. Furious, Churchill replied that he would pardon Stalin's remarks only on account of the bravery of the Russian army. Impressed with Churchill's spirit, Stalin mellowed, and the conference ended on a cordial note. On the plane ride from Moscow, Averell Harriman (who later became US Ambassador to the Soviet Union), scribbled a note to Churchill asking whether Stalin had accepted TORCH – the code name for the planned Allied landings in French North Africa. Churchill, who had met with Stalin privately just before they left, replied, "No, but he thinks it's absolutely right, and of great indirect advantage to Russia."

By November 1942, my grandfather had been promoted to Commodore 1st class, and was at the shore Naval Base in Algiers, named *HMS Hannibal*. He was directly involved in Operation Torch from 8th -16th November, and was responsible for berthing of convoys and getting ships out to sea again, in the shortest possible time. Algiers was a very busy port, and from all accounts, teeming with troops from every part of the Allied and Axis World. Before the operation began, the Americans and British organized Polish spies to gauge the feeling of the Vichy French forces, and make contact with those who would support the Allied invasion. As far as the British were concerned, French loyalties were always in question, as they were indeed to many ordinary Frenchmen, who were in an impossible situation. The idea of the operation was that they would attack simultaneously on three fronts Casablanca, Oran and Algiers.

On the 8th November, French Resistance fighters took over Algiers at midnight, seizing key targets including the telephone exchange, the radio station, the Governor's house and the headquarters of 19th Corps. The next day, British and American troops landed, and by evening, General Alphonse Juin, the senior Vichy French Army officer in North Africa, had surrendered the city to the Allies. This, however, did not stop the fighting because the Vichy Admiral, Darlan, also happened to be there at the time and added to the confusion between the Vichy and Free French forces. My grandfather's job was to take care of all the various factions and troops, some invading, others leaving. This was successful, but in appalling conditions – there was an outbreak of the plague and all the troops had to be inoculated. In the harbour on board ship, the sailors had to sleep in bunks with their feet in tins of paraffin to deter the bed bugs, and once the generators were shut down, huge rats would scurry along the mooring ropes on to the ship at night,

By February 1943 some order had been achieved, and a planning staff was formed in Algiers, under the joint command of Admiral Cunningham and U.S Admiral Hewitt. Admiral Cunningham, who had appointed my grandfather, said of him:

> "I saw much of him and his work. Algiers, which was our principal port for the supply of the Army and the

> repair of ships, was no bed of roses. Morse's conspicuous ability, his drive and energy, quiet imperturbability and charm of manner, coupled with his innate flair for getting the best out of people and getting on with all and sundry, particularly the French and Americans, were assets of great price which enabled him to succeed where many others might have failed."

In general, the War was taking a turn for the better. On November 29, 1942, Churchill addressed a worldwide radio audience. He described the successful American-led landings in Algeria and Morocco, and the defeat of Rommel by General Montgomery, at the second Battle of El Alamein. This meant the Allies were again in control in North Africa. He referred to the 'bright gleam of victory', and praised the 'perfect comradeship and understanding' between Anglo-American troops. He said North Africa was 'a springboard' facing 'the underside of subjugated Europe'. In this way, he swept away the American criticism of his preference for Mediterranean operations, instead of a more direct approach through northwest Europe into Germany. By the time of the Casablanca Conference (January 14th–24th 1943), Churchill had convinced Roosevelt of the effectiveness of an attack through, what he liked to call the 'under belly of the Axis'. They decided to continue with operations in the Mediterranean, once they had driven the Germans and Italians out of North Africa.

For his work in Algiers, my grandfather received the Officer's grade of the American Legion of Merit:

> 'For exceptionally meritorious conduct of a high degree in the performance of outstanding services. As Senior Officer in Charge of the Port of Algiers, Commodore Morse controlled the principle port of entry of British personnel and supplies arriving to support the Tunisian campaign. His skill and ingenuity in handling the vast amount of shipping from this port have been major factors in the successful supply of campaign troops in Tunisia.'

Chapter 25

Jane 1942

Phone for the fish knives, Norman
As cook is a little unnerved;
You kiddies have crumpled the serviettes
And I must have things daintily served.
John Betjeman "How to get on in Society"

While Commodore Morse was battling it out in the Mediterranean, my mother, Jane, was in Oxford. At some time in spring or early summer she met a clever young doctor, James Douglas, whom she married in a quick wartime marriage, looking happy and pretty, in an elegant white short-skirted suit. In her father's absence, Sir John Thornycroft, as the oldest friend of the family, gave her away. My grandmother's wedding present was a Baby Austin car, which had been first produced in 1922, with idea of 'motoring for the millions' and was cheap to run. Although she never talked about it to me, I imagine that my mother's marriage probably gave her freedom, self-assurance and love.

It gave her the chance to meet intellectuals and artists in the heady atmosphere of wartime Oxford. This was much more interesting than the round of deb dances she had soon bored of, and she started to lead a much more bohemian life than her more conventional childhood. Pretty and bright and, in her favour – not an intellectual – many fascinating clever men found her attractive. She was a breath of fresh air amongst the bluestockings.

Jane and James at their wedding

She enjoyed the attention, and when my brother and I were children, she would happily drop the names of all the people she knew, some of them obviously intimately. Some became life-long friends. There were the people from the Bloomsbury set, the Garnetts, Roger Fry, the Connolly's, the Huxley's and many others. She found their ideas and their artistic expression interesting, and they influenced her life and opinions at this time.

'Bourgeois' was a word my mother used often: something she and her friends were not. It was one of the most damning accusations she could make about a person or family. She admired the 'aristocracy', and the simple 'peasant' whose life she tried to emulate in her old age. In fact, I realize now that it was not just my mother, but a whole generation of intellectuals and artists to whom the 'bourgeois' were anathema – 'frightfully bourgeois, my dear.' I never quite knew what it meant, but it certainly meant 'boring and unimaginative, and solid.' It was people who strove to 'better themselves' in a slightly laughable way, because they somehow got it wrong, – satirized brilliantly in John Betjeman's poems like *'How to Get on in Society'*. More serious perhaps, was the influence of earlier writers like D.H. Lawrence, and poets like T.S. Eliot, who had become very popular in the 1930's, with poems like 'The Love Song of Alfred Prufrock' *"...Do I dare disturb the universe..."* Richard Wagner, with the foresight of a genius, portrayed the same traits even earlier in his opera, *"The Ring"*. The character of Fricka, the wife of Wotan, wanted to maintain the *status quo* at all costs. In the 1940's, this attitude to the 'beastly bourgeois' probably stemmed partly from the 'Fall of France' and the Vichy government. They were the epitome of the last stand of bourgeois Europe, with its characteristics of cowardice and opportunism. In many people's eyes, it was almost better to be Fascist or Communist, than bourgeois. The beginning of World War II and the fall of France ended the reign of the bourgeois inheritors of the French Revolution. Now, Petain's collaborative government in Vichy declared France must strive for: *'Travail, famille, patrie'* (work, family, fatherland); somehow even worse than the republican motto: *'Liberté, égalité, fraternité'*. My mother had close friends involved in the French Resistance; collaborators were not popular in England, where De Gaulle and his Free French were supported. Unlike my grandparents, she and her intellectual friends in Oxford were not trying to preserve a way of life, but rather rebelling and looking for new values to replace, what they considered, outmoded ideas. They were trying to make some sense of terrifying times in which they found themselves, and wondering about the future. Some of her friends were conscientious objectors; many did not believe in God, one of her closest friends at the time was a 'Logical

Positivist'. She even told me much later, she experimented with drugs. They lived life for each day as the Germans bombed England, and they did not know if they would live to see the next. They were rebelling against the very English gentlemanliness that most of the European bourgeoisie, even the Germans, admired and were still trying to emulate.

In the cold, snowy January of 1942 the first American troops arrived in the British Isles. Churchill wanted to concentrate the Navy and troops, for the time being, in the Mediterranean; so air power provided virtually the only means the Allies had to strike at Germany, and defend our shores. The Americans went into training, but they had plenty of time on their hands. It was six months to a year before they were to see any action. The Royal Air Force began its air offensive against Germany in May 1942, but it was not until 4th July that the first American crews participated in air raids against the Continent.

The presence of American GI's was to change Britain as much as the War. The Americans with their peculiar brand of charm – warm and spontaneous – were able to thaw British traditional reserve; their generosity became legendary. They sympathized with children deprived of chocolate and candy by the War; theirs was not the British attitude of 'seen and not heard'. They responded with comics and special children's parties, where their young guests simply could not believe the mounds of food available. Some units adopted orphaned British children for a year and provided treats, outings, clothes, toys and other delights. Women, ground down by the drabness and make-do-and-mend of wartime life, found they were no less lavish. Unfortunately, some of the GIs were unable to identify those girls who were out to plunder them for all they could get. A bulging wallet, nylons, silk scarves and other luxuries provided by the PX Stores were not the only reason for the lure Americans exerted over British women. The greatest attraction was their courtly approach. In contrast to the average frosty British male, the Americans knew how to make a girl feel good. Their opening gambit - "Hello, Duchess!" or "Hiya, beautiful!" - sounded "fresh" at first, but the troubadour treatment that followed dazzled women unused to such gentility. Of course the men did not appreciate the GIs in the same way, and the common British jibe about them was that they were, "overfed, overpaid and over here".

By the end of the War, however, the American influence had changed British attitudes in many ways. The antipathy had been upended. Many British, who had once accepted their miserable, but inevitable, lot during the pre-War deprivations – class distinctions, mass unemployment, miserly welfare, slum housing, bad health, bad diet – began to rethink their place in life. In the years after the War it was soon proved that attitudes had changed fundamentally. It was the GIs, with their ideas about personal freedom and opportunity for all, who played a major role in bringing about a much more optimistic mindset, which started to blow Britain apart in the 1960's.

My mother always had the ability to move between diverse worlds. She was at ease with intellectuals as she was with gardeners, farmers and charladies. Like many other women she fell for the American charm and fun. In a general feeling that they might only survive another day, many marriages were doomed for failure. My mother did what many people at that time were doing – she was unfaithful and slept around, and in 1944, she realized she was pregnant. Rather than have an abortion, which was not really an easy option in those days, she decided to do what she thought was honourable and ask James for a divorce. She never spoke about James, she perhaps felt bad about the way she had treated him. He was probably too nice and bored my mother. They must have remained on reasonable terms though, as I remember him coming to visit when I was about four in London. He was a kind and mild man whom I had decided to hate, and I hid in a cupboard and pelted him with old toast. He did not deserve such treatment.

In spite of her bravado, she was probably devastated by the pregnancy, and more so, by her mother's rejection of her, at a time when she could have done with support. My grandmother and Mary, in their embarrassment, took a Victorian stance, something for which my mother never really forgave them. They behaved very badly and banished her to a pregnancy alone in a house outside Oxford, and would have nothing to do with her. For my grandmother, it was probably the last straw, so soon after Clyde's death. By the time I was born they seemed to have come to some sort of compromise, as there were photographs of my mother, with me in a pram at Chute, with my grandmother and Nan looking doting. This was not long before D Day in May 1945 when I was a few months old, safely in the country and away from London and the bombs. Almost certainly my grandmother could not resist the temptation of having a relationship with her granddaughter. Later, when I was older, she supplied no end of treats and support, like riding lessons, pantomimes and eventually paid for my public school. I genuinely loved her.

My Grandmother and I at Bembridge

But the rift became worse and was never really forgotten. Three years later when my brother was conceived, in the south of

France by a different father, my grandmother, with Mary's support, tried to adopt me. I realize with hindsight that my mother was quite magnanimous, allowing my brother and I to go and visit as much as we did. My grandmother and Mary always did a lot of hinting and made much of wondering who was my father. This is when I delved into the secrets of Whistler's Chinese cabinet, which my great-grandfather Sydney Morse had bought so many years ago. I found some pictures and sometimes tackled my mother on the taboo subject but she always replied that she did not know. It was not James – it was either a Jewish philosopher, or an American GI with whom she had a one-night stand. In the end I decided I did not resemble the Jewish philosopher much, so I plumped for the American, of whom there was no photograph, and who could be whatever I imagined.

Either way, it was blot on my childhood, especially when I was sent to a very conventional boarding school and I had to answer to curious little schoolmates, who all seemed to have fathers in Oil, Business or Politics. I would say my mother was divorced and then, when the bolder ones pressed on past that disgrace (it was not as normal as it is today) as to what he did, I was stumped as to what to say. If I had not felt so vulnerable, I probably could have had a good time inventing fathers, but I did not have the wit for that. I would usually answer with an evasive "I don't know", and in the end they would sense the awkwardness and leave me alone.

My mother was extremely courageous, much braver than I. The grumpy young woman whom my grandmother had described on the trip to China was gone forever. She had a strong impact on my character and upbringing, perhaps even more so since both my brother and I had grown up with no father. A complicated character, I did not really appreciate her until I had my own children and was surer of myself, which was after she had died an early death at the age of 60.

She was very outgoing and friendly – someone with whom people instantly felt at ease, in fact many of my friends became closer to her than me. Some of her past pupils in the villages in Somerset and Dorset remembered her with fondness, as an inspirational art teacher. As a mother, she was very loving and warm – I never felt neglected or unloved. At the same time she could be incredibly naïve and gullible to a critical child's eyes. I did, however, hold against her the fact that she never provided us with a father, or any male in the household when we were growing up, except of course her friend, the delightful Orlando, but he was hardly a male influence. He was a ballet dancer and the 'female' side of a happily 'married', what was then called 'queer', couple. We loved Orlando and his whippet; he would tap dance for us and was sweet to us when our mother got angry. But in general I felt responsible, rather as if I had to be the 'grown up', and it was the three of us against the world.

Jane never seemed daunted by difficulty or poverty. She certainly had the insurance policy of her father somewhere in the background supporting her, but she would daringly launch into things at which other people would have baulked. When I was about ten and desperately wanted a pony (I prayed for one fervently every night and we still lived in London), she somehow got the money. I think she may have won something betting on horses, which she did from time to time, or she may have sold some paintings. We all drove, in one day, out to Sir Anthony Eden's daughter's house in Bagshot, and bought my first pony 'Ghazal', and a companion for him 'Blackcurrant Bun'. The same day we bought a Landrover and horsebox, and then drove them to Feltham Waterworks where we rented a field for them; it is now part of Heathrow Airport. We had happy times riding there. But I am jumping ahead of the story.

Chapter 26

The Liberation of Naples

"When he designs the assault in his mind he is alone cut off from everyone. He is alone in the moonlight and the crowded men about him are strangers in time"
John Steinbeck - 'Once There was a War'

On July 9th-10th 1943, with almost no resistance, convoys of American and Allied troops moved north from Malta into Sicily, in a very smooth operation named Operation Husky. The night was stormy and the Sicilians were sleeping soundly, thinking that nobody in his right mind would attack in such weather. They were anyway tired of war, and not keen on the Germans. The Allies had prepared the way in secret negotiations, as they had done in Algiers, to persuade the Italians to give up the fight and join them. On July 24th Mussolini was asked to step down by King Victor Emanuel, and Marshal Pietro Badoglia replaced him.

After Algiers, my grandfather's next stop was the island resort of Capri. He arrived on 13th August 1943. General Eisenhower, now Supreme Allied Commander in the Mediterranean, arrived the next day, in an American destroyer to take possession of the island.

Anthony with Eisenhower

My grandfather was promoted to Rear Admiral, and Governor of the island. He appointed the senior Italian officer as temporary commander of the garrison, and Guiseppe Brindisi as mayor, and warned that any manifestations of fascism would be severely punished. He imposed a curfew from eight at night until six in the morning and forbade night fishing and bathing. He and his staff rounded up refugees and housed those in need until their eventual evacuation. His headquarters was the Villa Ciano, the luxurious summer home of Edda Ciano, Mussolini's glamorous daughter, married to his ex-foreign minister, Ciano. It must have been welcome after the squalor of Algiers. They took over Ciano's staff and benefited from the fine food and wine they found in the abandoned house. The villa was on top of one of the two high hills, with spectacular views of the Bay of Naples and Vesuvius, smoking in the background; from there they could observe the comings and goings in the Bay without being noticed. It was a waiting game, but must have been a welcome brief respite. Amongst the Americans there at the same time were Lt Commander Douglas Fairbanks Jr USNR, and John Steinbeck, who was correspondent for the New York Times; also there was the British writer and spy, Ian Fleming, who wrote about his time there in his book about the war, 'Commandos'. Another visitor at the time was Harold Macmillan, and his wife.

By August 17th 40,000 German and 60,000 Italian troops were evacuated from Sicily, and in the words of General Alexander, the British Deputy Commander, the 'last German soldier was flung out'. On 3rd September the Italian government agreed to an Armistice with the Allies. The British Army landed on the 'toe' of Italy and the Armistice was publicly announced on the 8th September. On the 9th the Americans landed at Salerno. They expected little resistance, but were surprised that there were still German troops, who had not yet withdrawn and who put up a strong fight. They then centred on the port of Naples, selected because it was the northernmost port that could receive Allied air support by fighter aircraft operating from Sicily.

On the ground, in Naples, it was a different story. From the time of the Italian government's Armistice and the Allied landings, the city had become the scene of complete confusion, terrible civil rioting and siege; many people not knowing which side they were on. Prisoners of war and Italian troops converged on Naples adding to the chaos. On October 1st 1943 the Americans and Allied troops arrived and my grandfather's work was to begin, sorting out the confusion. This was something at which he excelled. There is a photograph of my grandfather in the middle of the first chaos of Naples, directing prisoners-of-war.

Anthony (right) sorting out prisoners of war in Naples

He worked hard with Commodore W.A. Sullivan USN to get the port functioning again, removing magnetic mines from the approach waters. On 30th October he was made Flag Officer for Western Italy, and assigned to *HMS Hasdrubal*. One compatriot later describing his work said:

> "The genius of the Naples dockyard was British Rear Admiral J.A.V Morse. In cooperation with the American army and a dozen other armies represented in Italy, he kept men and goods in constant movement northward to the front line and reasonably safe from looters."

The Sydney Herald published, later in the War, praised his work saying:

> "Rear-Admiral J. A. V. Morse has had great experience in the rehabilitation of captured areas, ranging from Algiers to Naples. At Naples, for instance, he created a port which was able to handle more traffic than New York."

In 1944, in June he was on an official visit to Bastia, Corsica with Admiral Hewitt, United States Navy; in July he had a private audience with the Pope at the Vatican. On 24th July 1944, King George

VI visited Naples and my grandfather was appointed his ADC for the visit. The King was a considerate and pragmatic man, who was more interested in the business of royalty than its trappings. He was proving to be a brave and inspiring wartime leader, with a great sympathy for the people of the Armed Forces. He tried to spend as much of his time as possible with them, encouraging, visiting battlegrounds and inspecting the troops. He and his wife, Queen Elizabeth, were determined to modernize their role and make it more acceptable to the common man. They were anxious to steer an even course that would survive the trials of war, revolutions and modern life.

Rear Admiral Morse and King George VI, Naples

The two men had much in common – both had had the same training at Osborne, Dartmouth and the Navy, they were almost the same age and both firm believers in duty. Probably that was as far as the comparison went, but it was enough for my grandmother, who put this picture proudly in her album.

Gradually my grandfather restored order to Naples and the ports of Western Italy, which were used to transfer machinery and ammunition to the troops. By the winter of 1944 things became relatively calm. It became clear the Allies were winning. He stayed in Italy until June 1945 when he hauled down his flag and left for England. His work there was widely acclaimed.

> "He was awarded the American Medal of Freedom for exceptionally meritorious conduct in the performance of outstanding services in Italy and Southern France from September 1943 to June 1945. As Flag Officer Western Italy, and later as Flag Officer, Northern Area, Mediterranean, Rear-Admiral Morse controlled the movement, routing, and acceptance of all vessels of all nationalities entering Western Italian ports and adjacent waters. He was responsible for all escort vessels and made final decisions on protective and security measures for all vessels in the area under his command. Since the success of the operations in Italy and the invasion of Southern France depended upon waterborne movement of supplies and personnel his responsibilities were exceedingly great. Through his efficient organization and unflagging efforts these water movements and port discharges were made with only infinitesimal losses, thereby enabling the Allied Armies to overwhelm the enemy with superior might bringing the successful termination of the War at an earlier date."

Chapter 27

The End of War

In August 1944 the British and American armies invaded France from north, west and south in a huge push. Paris was liberated on the 25th. The War finally came to an end with Hitler's suicide on 30th April 1945, and Germany signed an unconditional surrender on May 7th. Victory in Europe Day was celebrated on the 8thMay. Crowds of jubilant people came out onto the streets in London, especially in front of Buckingham Palace, where the King and Queen appeared on the balcony with their daughters Elizabeth and Margaret, to wave to the cheers of their subjects. Winston Churchill was invited to join them, the first time in history that non-royalty was included in such an occasion. It was a proud moment for Churchill. There were street parties all over the country on village greens, and bonfires illuminated the bombsites. The celebrations were slightly overshadowed by the fact that Japan had still not surrendered. Early in July, there was a general election resulting in a landslide victory for the Labour Party, and Clement Attlee became Prime Minister. The English wanted change and the chance to create the social state they had thought of before the War.

When the War ended my grandfather's work for the Navy was not quite finished. On 6th August 1945 American airmen dropped an atomic bomb on Hiroshima, followed by one on Nagasaki on 9th August. It was a sobering sign of the shape of things to come. Six days later, Japan announced its surrender to the Allies, signing the Instrument of Surrender on 2nd September, officially ending World War

II. All of August, after the atom bomb was dropped, my grandfather had waited in Calcutta preparing. The Japanese capitulated on September 5th at dawn, and *HMS Kedah* was the first ship to arrive in Singapore. My grandfather was on board as Rear Admiral Malaya Designate, with his combined operations staff, senior officers of the British military and the chairman of the Singapore harbour. It was described as 'a dramatic moment'. For three years a secret staff had been working on plans to be put into operation when Singapore was reoccupied. My grandfather took over the base, and with his great experience in the rehabilitation of captured areas did a splendid job, highly praised by the syndicated press.

> "A floating dock of 50,000 tons has been built in India in anticipation of damage to the dry dock at Singapore, for which a complete spare caisson is being constructed. More than 100 ratings, manning a self-contained mobile radio station are ready to land, and other complete units built and prepared in India ready to operate instantly include oil tanks and a pipeline system, a water purification plant; a landing craft base, with laundry, canteen, and cinema; a naval air base, with cranes, tools, stores, and accommodation; hutments; canteens, with a mobile bakery and refrigerators; also fitted in America as floating electric power plants. More than 500 specialist repair ratings and a battalion of Royal Marines are waiting to move in to restore the port facilities. Rear-Admiral Morse has had great experience in the rehabilitation of damaged harbours, including Naples, where in a short time he created a port able to handle more traffic than New York."

On 18th December 1945 my grandfather's work was honoured. He was made a Knight of the British Empire, (KBE). From then on he was known as Vice Admiral Sir Anthony Morse, and my grandmother, as Lady Morse, a title she enjoyed. He retired, much decorated from the Navy in 1947. He was 55.

My grandfather

Titles and Medals
Great War Gallipoli "V.C. action" D.S.O. gallantry during the River Clyde action off 'V' Beach in April 1915
Jubilee 1935, Coronation 1937
C.B. to his honours for the evacuation of Crete in 1941
The Most Honourable Order of the Bath, C.B.
British War and Victory Medals, M.I.D.
1939-45 Atlantic Star, Africa Star, Burma Star, Italy Star
War Medal 1939-45
United States of America, Legion of Merit,
France, Legion of Honour, Officer's breast badge

France, Croix de Guerre 1939
United States of America, Medal of Freedom
China (Republic) Order of the Brilliant Jade
Algiers Chamber of Commerce, silver medallion, the edge inscribed 'Monsieur le Contre-Amiral Morse, Flag Office, Algeria, 1943'
Senior Flag Officer in the Mediterranean 1943-45 and was elevated to K.B.E.
C.B.E. for his part in Operation "Shingle" (London Gazette 6 June 1944 refers)

For a while he took a job at Rediffusion, which had previously manufactured naval telecommunications equipment, and after the War became the Independent Television Association. Living in London again, he must have wondered what there was in England for him. After so many years away in foreign lands and the excitement of the high seas, working at Rediffusion turned out to be a confined box, a prison that he did not enjoy. He was not cut out for work in an office, however innovative the ideas of television and communications were. He must have also missed the sun. The dreary, damp weather of England got into his bones and, furthermore, it was no longer the place he remembered when he was growing up. He lived most of the time either in the flat in Halkin Place, or at his club in London, with visits to us when he read us stories.

My grandparents must have accepted, at some point, the sad fact that the War had devastated, not only the way of life they had known in their youth, but their personal lives together. They came to an arrangement. The home they had dreamed of before the War seemed to have no point; the children were gone and my grandmother had made a life for herself with Mary. They decided to sell Chute Collis. She chose to live at the Shepherds Cottage, on the outskirts of the village of Upper Chute. They had already bought the place before Clyde had been so tragically killed, as a home to which Mary could retire. She and Mary lived in small huts again while they were converting the cottage into a suitable place for them both. They bought a plot of land the other side of the village green and built another small wooden house, in which Mary's school friend, Rosellen, could live and be their cook. Nan went to live in a council house in Battersea to look after her aging father. My brother and I visited my grandmother, during school holidays, either at Chute, or the bungalow she built in Bembridge, the place that held so many fond memories for her. She was a supplier of expensive treats my mother could not afford at that time in the 1950's, when rationing for many things was still in force. My friends called her "Lady Ginger Pop", as ginger beer was one of the treats she offered at croquet and quoits parties. There were outings to the pantomime in London, when she hired a box and rented a chauffer- driven Rolls Royce to ferry us there, or we would go for high tea at The Goring Hotel. She settled into a comfortable old age, with Mary and Rosellen waiting on her, a simple life with the luxuries she enjoyed.

My early childhood was spent in London, in the rather dreary 1950's. The bombsites behind our flat in Soho served as playgrounds; on the other hand, children could play in the streets with no fear of danger, everyone left their doors unlocked and there were plenty of jobs. People were still very formal, and conformed to social mores. Most men still wore hats and suits to work, beards were thought terribly bohemian; I remember my grandmother making jokes about some of my mother's friends who had beards, calling them 'prawns'. The Feminist movement did not start until the 1960's, with people like Betty Friedman and German Greer. Women in the 50's were still being encouraged to be perfect housewives of increasingly small families; the brunt of heavy advertising campaigns, to make their homes more efficient and beautiful, and to buy things on the 'never never', as hire purchase (credit) was then called. I have to say, much to my chagrin as a child, my mother never fitted into this mould. I went through a stage of wanting a perfect bourgeois mother, like my little Italian friend up the road, with satin curtains and frills on everything.

In 1956 the film of 'The River Plate', starring Peter Finch as Captain Langsdorff, was premiered to a very popular response. My grandfather must have collaborated on the script, as he appears in the credits. Clyde is mentioned; when the *Graf Spee* first shells the *Exeter* someone says: "Was that Morse?" He must have done this work as a final tribute to Clyde. He decided to go and live in Rhodesia and look for uranium – the latest adventure and a way to make money in the coming nuclear age. For better or worse, England after two World Wars had changed out of recognition. He did not live long enough to witness the full impact, but the English went from being colonialists with a great Empire, whom people wanted to emulate, to individuals on a small pink island, not even properly part of Europe. He bought a small farm in Ruwa, outside Salisbury, and went and settled there. It probably reminded him of the happy times he had had with Clyde in South Africa.

My grandfather on his farm in Rhodesia

I was by now 11 years old and about to go to Sherborne School for Girls. By selling what remained of her lease on the flat in London, and with some help from my grandfather, my mother bought a smallholding Bembury Farm, in Dorset. It was within easy bicycling distance from Sherborne – about 4 miles, and so my brother and I could go daily to good schools, without the exorbitant fees of boarding. Always game for a new challenge, my mother took up farming and growing vegetables, with the help of books and advice from an old codger. We took the three ponies that were still in the Waterworks in Feltham. It was a perfect childhood in many ways, although it was hard work. We helped to look after the animals, milked the cows, went to gymkhanas, pony club and hunt balls. There were blissful summers making hay with the sweet smells of the drying grass, driving the tractor and using all one's strength to haul up the bales. At the end of the day we would could canter round the field on the new stubble and jump the ponies over the piled up bales – strictly forbidden, and therefore so much fun. We would fall into bed and sleep the deep contented sleep of physical labourers. We picked fruit, bottled it and made jam.

Then, on 7th May 1960, my grandfather was killed when his motor bicycle collided with a bus, not far from his farm in Ruwa. He was sixty-eight. My mother was devastated by the news. It was only at that point that I became aware of her vulnerability and loneliness. Even though my grandfather had spent relatively little time with her, he was her hero and her anchor. I would hear her weeping at night. I was not accustomed to my strong and resourceful mother's frailty and it frightened me. My reaction to the news was that I ran up the lane to the village church, in the dark. Even though I was by now fifteen, I was still terribly afraid of the dark and too frightened to go down the path past the grave stones, so I prayed outside the perimeter of the graveyard, deciding God would hear me just as well outside the Church. I prayed that God would take care of her, because I could not. I think He did.

My grandfather requested in his Will, that his ashes were scattered over the place where the Battle of the River Plate had been fought, so the Royal Navy obliged and did this honour for him. He was finally reunited with his beloved Clyde. Not long after this, when I was sixteen I left home and started my own life in London; with the selfishness of youth I soon forgot my mother's loneliness. I had my own way to make in the world and I was no longer interested in my family. My grandmother helped me in many ways at the beginning, paying for a secretarial course and my first lodgings, and sending food parcels that would arrive in a green Harrods van every week. She died peacefully in her own bed one night in 1968. She was 79.

The times exploded into the swinging sixties with hippies and flower-power. We had all had enough of austerity and Britain was cool, booming and fun.

Postcript

"Give relatives their due..."
Qur'an

My story is at an end now. It ends, as it began, in a desert, but this time a different one in North Africa, a desert full of roses. The ancient mud houses have people living in them. There are mountains in the distance full of snow that melts in the spring and gives water. This is a benign land, not harsh, and the people are full of love and welcome.

It is almost 50 years since I first embarked on my journey as a Muslim. At first, with the ardour of conversion, I thought all my family and old friends were non-believers and, quite cruelly, I had very little to do with them. They had too strong an influence on me and, although I loved them, I stayed away. It is only now that I begin to understand them. I realize they were good, decent, people who struggled with their lives in cataclysmic conditions, and their history is part of who I am. They followed what they believed in – however erroneous I might consider it – King and Country, the Empire, Duty; values that in the light of today's anarchy seem not so bad after all. I found my own way, but I could not blame them for what they did not know. They died defending their beliefs and for that they were heroes. I have come to know my grandparents, and my mother, more intimately than I ever knew them when they were alive, and my uncle whom I never knew, is now a living memory. I know now that they were believers, but did not have what we Muslims call *'deen'* – life-transaction, a way of translating belief into daily life, with the *'sunna'* – the habits of the

Prophet Muhammad, peace be upon him. The Christian religion, in which they had been brought up, no longer provided that. I once asked my mother, who accepted my conversion happily, if she believed in God and she said 'Yes', but she did not believe in religion, she believed in God in Creation; what I would call His Attributes. I like to think that my grandfather heard the call to prayer being recited in the minarets in Algiers, Beirut and Alexandria, and perhaps it struck a chord in his heart.

Family life and values have changed out of recognition since my grandparent's time. Most of the world is in debt. Morocco and many other Muslim countries are considered Third world countries, but is England any better off? Here, in the desert, people still live the *deen* of Allah in its simple, pure form. They are generous and hospitable, they beat drums and sing praises of the Prophet, peace be upon him, to ancient rhythms. Perhaps the whole debacle will pass them by, but many of the younger people here have gone off to work or be educated in the 'richer First world', and find themselves in ghettos far worse than the homes they left behind. Some are discovering that perhaps the life they had here is better than the 'West' and have returned. Others make desperate attempts to defend an Islam that they hardly know, as they have had no traditional education in their *deen.* I say this because I think it is, sadly, what happens to young Muslims and converts who join terrorist groups; they want to fight for a cause, belong to a community and put right what they see as the injustices the Muslims suffer. Often, the only way they can experience 'brotherhood' is in terrorist camps. We British, including, I'm sorry to say, Lawrence of Arabia whom I admired, along with other colonials like the French, have a lot to answer for in the changes to the traditional Muslim way of life, by imposing our western education and financial system upon them. Modern life and education have changed us all and we cannot put back the clock, but we need to address these issues and come to a better understanding. But then, there have always been threats from the 'other'; in my grandparent's time it was Fascism, later it was Communism, now, unhappily, it is Islam.

I look at my hands as they age and recall my grandmother's hands. I knew them so well as a child, slightly gnarled and dappled with age spots; they are familiar. I do not have the gnarling rheumatic lumps, my vitamins probably staved that off, but perhaps that will come. The hands are hers and mine. My family are a part of my make up, but they are not me. I have come to realize that, part of knowing myself, is knowing what I have inherited; to be proud of it and then I can let it go, a little wiser about who I am, with forgiveness for their faults and my own. There is a certain time in life when one inevitably rejects one's family. Later in life, with more discrimination, one is able to appreciate and be thankful to the people who formed such an important part of that life. Perhaps now I can put all the ghosts of my ancestors to rest, with gratefulness for who they were and what they struggled through, and how they indirectly brought me to Islam.

May they all rest in peace!

The desert rolls over all the memories, cleaning the slate in the same way my son tells me he does, every morning when he has learnt a piece of Qur'an. He washes it clean and then writes the next *ayats* (verses from the Qur'an) he has to learn. It is good to look forward to the future, whatever it may bring. It has been a long journey and it is not finished yet. I have witnessed my children and their friends grow up as Muslims, and bring a new dynamic European flavour to Islam, which is not violent in any way. They obviously have their own struggles but they are mostly inward, what the Sufis call 'the greater *jihad'* – that of the self. I have seen many people with family stories like my own, become Muslim. I have seen the children of traditional Muslim families, which they have rejected, become interested in Islam again because of what we showed them; what, for them had become a family religion full of outdated traditions, was suddenly interesting and made sense in a modern age.

I thank Allah for that and for His many gifts to me.

"Mankind! Have taqwa (fearful awareness) of your Lord and fear a day when no father will be able to atone for his son,
or son for his father, in any way.
Allah's promise is true.
So do not let the life of the dunya** (this world) **delude you
And do not let the Deluder delude you concerning Allah.
Truly Allah has knowledge of the Hour, and He sends down abundant rain and knows what is in the womb.
And no self knows what it will earn tomorrow; and no self knows in what land it will die;
Allah is All-Knowing, All-Aware"
(Quran 31:32) Translated by Abdalhaqq and Aisha Bewley

About Amelia Morse

Amelia Morse is the granddaughter of Rear Admiral Sir Anthony Morse and Lady Marly Morse.

Amelia currently lives in Spain but has travelled and lived all over the world – England, Morocco, America, Scotland and South Africa. She has been a teacher, jeweller, and at one time ran a weaving shop in Norwich, England.

The author

Thanks and Acknowledgements

My thanks are to my Shaykh

And to all those who helped me in so many ways,

and specifically with this book

My family

My brother Charles, and his wife Emma

Abdal Basir Ojembarrena

Mansurah Mears

Aisha Wright

Tahira Jayes

Ahmad Abdalhayy Pastor

Contacts

ameliamorse@sifipublishing.co.uk

info@sifipublishing.co.uk

SIFIPUBLISHING

WWW.SIFIPUBLISHING.CO.UK

www.sifipublishing.co.uk

Lightning Source UK Ltd.
Milton Keynes UK
UKOW06f1915190415

249934UK00007B/92/P

9 781910 088265